THE SECOND EVANGELICAL AWAKENING

Also by J. Edwin Orr

CAN GOD—?
FULL SURRENDER
THE SECOND EVANGELICAL AWAKENING IN AMERICA
THE SECOND EVANGELICAL AWAKENING IN BRITAIN

*This book is an abridgment in more popular
style of the author's two theses—The Second
Evangelical Awakening in America and The
Second Evangelical Awakening in Britain*

THE
SECOND EVANGELICAL AWAKENING

An account of the Second *Worldwide* Evangelical
Revival beginning in the Mid-Nineteenth Century

by
J. EDWIN ORR

Master of Arts (Northwestern), Doctor of Philosophy (Oxford),
Doctor of Theology (Northern), Member of the American Historical
Association, Fellow of the Royal Historical Society, etc.

Originally Published by
MARSHALL, MORGAN & SCOTT
LONDON & EDINBURGH

LONDON
MARSHALL, MORGAN & SCOTI, LTD.
33 LUDGATE HILL, E.C.4

AUSTRALIA & NEW ZEALAND
317 COLLINS STREET
MELBOURNE

SOUTH AFRICA
P.O. BOX 1720, STURK'S BUILDINGS
CAPE TOWN

U.S.A.
VAN KAMPEN PRESS
222 E AST WILLOW STREET
WHEATON, ILLINOIS

CANADA
EVANGELICAL PUBLISHERS
366 BAY STREET
TORONTO

First (unabridged) Edition 1949
First (popular) Edition 1955

MADE AND PRINTED JN GREAT BRITAIN BY PURNELL AND SONS, LTD.
PAULTON (SOMERSET) AND LONDON

Republished 2018 by Enduring Word
ISBN: 978-1-939466-43-3
Copied from the first popular edition
With permission from the family of the late Dr. J. Edwin Orr
Resources from Dr. J. Edwin Orr may be found at:
www.jedwinorr.com

FOREWORD

WHEN Chaplain J. Edwin Orr returned from service in the Pacific with the U.S. Air Force it was with the intention of proceeding to Oxford and there writing a history of the Great Awakening of the nineteenth century. Knowing his successful ministry in local awakenings around the world, and being aware of the burden of his heart for world-wide Revival and of his gift for writing attractively on such matters, we looked forward with great anticipation to the completion of his research.

At Oxford he won the coveted degree of Doctor of Philosophy, and later the Royal Historical Society and the Royal Society of Literature elected him to Fellowships.

We have had the privilege of publishing both the theses which won him his Doctor of Theology in the U.S.A. and his Doctor of Philosophy in Britain.

This latter book—*The Second Evangelical Awakening in Britain*—was immediately acclaimed a most useful book, and we have seldom known such unanimity of approval from the Christian and secular press reviewers. It was designated in *The Church of England Newspaper* as one of the ten most significant books published in Britain in that year.

The present book is a popular abridgment from the contents of both theses. The abridgment has been made in a desire to produce a book for widespread circulation. The originals were well authenticated with footnotes compiled with painstaking industry, and any scholar desiring to study the authorities quoted may do so by referring to the larger works.

It has been said that much of the current interest in the twentieth-century awakening in America and Britain can be ascribed to the appearance of these works, and Edwin Orr, having thus made his contribution, immediately threw himself into the work of promoting prayer for an increase in this interest which would lead to World Revival. America's leading evangelist has written of his work among colleges and churches in 1949 and 1950 in glowing terms: "I think that God has given him one of the greatest and most unique ministries anywhere in the nation"—a thought which has been echoed in American and Canadian periodicals by others than Billy Graham.

In 1950 Dr. Orr went to Brazil, and the General Secretary of the Church Confederation there reported a great movement of the Spirit unparalleled in the history of that country. Dr. Orr has since visited South Africa, where his campaign was supported by the Archbishop of Cape Town, the Moderators of the Dutch Reformed and Presbyterian Churches, and the Presidents of the Methodist Conference, the Baptist Union and the Congregational Union. During that time there were widespread signs of an awakening, and many students professed conversion.

It is our hope that the publication of this popular edition may contribute to the present interest in world-wide Revival.

PUBLISHERS.

Alec E. Rowlands

CONTENTS

AUTHOR'S INTRODUCTION

IN 1945, the author was pacing along a beach-head in the Pacific following a heavy air-raid, wondering whether or not he would survive the war. That night came a strange assurance from God that his life would be spared for a two-fold purpose—to become a historian of the great Nineteenth-Century Awakening, hitherto unchronicled, and to be an eye-witness of the beginnings of the Twentieth-Century Awakening, long desired. At the conclusion of hostilities, he hitch-hiked from Tokyo to Oxford via Capetown, some 24,000 miles. His volume, *The Second Evangelical Awakening*, is the outcome of that endeavour.

Already the author's designation *The Second Evangelical Awakening* is accepted by scholars in Britain. In the United States, there have been many periods of Revival—the New Jersey Revival under Freylinghuysen, the Pennsylvania Revival under the Tennents, the Virginia Revival among the Baptists, the New England Revival under Edwards, the Great Awakening under Whitefield, the Revival of 1800, the Revivals under Finney, the Western Revivals of the 1830's, the 1858 Awakening, the Revivals under Moody, Chapman, Torrey, Sunday and others. Only two of these movements became world-wide, *The Evangelical Revival of the Eighteenth Century*, and *the Evangelical Awakening of the Nineteenth Century beginning in 1858*. So, although the localized

Frontier Revival of 1800 is often called the Second Great Awakening in relation to the Great Awakening of 1840, the author chose the title of the present work in relation to its world-wide scope—*The Second* World-wide *Evangelical Awakening*.

Thanks are due to Professors Peder Stiansen and Faris Whitesell of Northern Baptist Theological Seminary in Chicago, and to history professors in other seminaries in the Chicago area, including Professor William Warren Sweet of the University of Chicago, under whom the author took a course in American Church History. Indebtedness is gratefully acknowledged to the Regius Professor of Ecclesiastical History in the University of Oxford, the Rev. Claude Jenkins, under whose supervision much of the work was accomplished. Thanks are also due to Geoffrey Williams, Librarian of the Evangelical Library in London, for extraordinary favours.

This volume presents a factual account of a truly remarkable spiritual awakening, which, taking its rise in Canada and the United States, spread all over the English-speaking world, adding two million new converts to the churches. The general conclusion is that this outbreak of revival ushered in a great Awakening in the nineteenth century which lasted fifty years, and is comparable in scope and effects with its forerunner, the Evangelical Revival of the eighteenth century.

CHAPTER ONE

THE SOURCES OF THE REVIVAL

IN THE middle of the nineteenth century, religious life in the United States of America was in decline. There were many reasons for the decline, political and social as well as religious. Political strife provoked tremendous interest everywhere. The slavery question was of paramount importance, and men's passions and energies were being diverted into the channels of contention on either side of the controversy.

Financial and commercial prosperity had an adverse effect upon the American people of the mid-century. The accessions of large areas as the spoils of the Mexican War, together with the discovery of gold in California, led to a wave of prosperity all over the nation. The zeal of the people was devoted to the accumulation of wealth, and other things, including religion, took a lesser place. Boom times caught the public fancy, and turned men's hearts from God.

Many people at the time lost faith in spiritual things because of the extremes of the Millerite apocalyptists. William Miller and others set a date for the return of our Lord to earth (April 23, 1843), deceiving many so thoroughly that they sold their effects and waited the Coming on the hilltops. Multitudes neglected their work, and certain wealthy people sold their goods and gave to the poor. The day arrived, and not a thing of extraordinary interest occurred. Public confidence became shaken, excitement died down, some deluded victims became bitter infidels, others adopted materialism, and quite a number were spoiled for Christian service. So widespread was the delusion that the churches generally became the subjects of ridicule, and public faith in religion was impaired. Between 1845 and 1855, there were several years in which the number of church accessions scarcely kept pace with the losses due to death and discipline.

These secular and religious conditions combined to bring about a crash. The third great panic in American history swept the giddy structure of speculative wealth away. Factories were shut down, and vast numbers thrown out of employment, New York City alone having thirty thousand idle men. In October, 1857, the hearts of the people were thoroughly weaned from speculation and uncertain gain, for despair stared them in the face. A year later a Dutch Reformed divine commented:

"But does adversity always lead men to God? Is it not, alas, common to see both individuals and communities acting after the example of that wicked king of old, of whom the emphatic record runs, 'And in the time of his distress did he trespass yet more against the Lord: this is that king, Ahaz.' Besides, in the year 1837, there was a commercial revulsion, quite as widespread and unexpected as that of 1857, and tenfold more disastrous; yet there was then no unusual turning to religion, no mighty movement of the popular mind, no upheaving of the foundations. The people as a whole were far more intent upon examining into the political or economic causes of the pecuniary pressure, than into its spiritual bearings, or its final cause as ordained in the providence of God."

Bishop Candler added his word: "And now that the wheels of industry stood still, and the noisy cries of greed were hushed, men stopped to hear the voice of the Spirit calling them to repentance. And they heeded the call."

For the beginnings of the religious revival which was soon to flood the United States, it is necessary to look beyond the borders of the Union. The first unusual stream of blessing arose in the city of Hamilton, in the Province of Ontario, known as Canada West. The sturdy settlers of the Ontarian peninsula were descendants of the United Empire Loyalists driven from their homes in the Thirteen Colonies. The first generation bred on Canadian soil had repelled by force of arms the attempt of the "war hawks" to acquire their territory for the powerful Union south of them. But they permitted peaceful American influences to invade Upper Canada. Methodism imported from the States exercised an influence far beyond its numerical strength, and was able to challenge the ascendancy of the Anglican Communion, protected as the latter was. From the beginning, these Canadian Methodists (like their Baptist fellow-citizens) were extremely evangelistic.

It was among the Ontarian Methodists that the first fruits of the 1858 revival occurred. The Methodist *Christian Advocate and Journal* of New York carried on November 5, 1857, a prominent headline *Revival Extraordinary* on its front page, with a sub-title which declared that from three to four hundred souls had been saved in a few days. Twenty-one persons had professed conversion on the first day of the movement and, as the work steadily increased, the number of public professions grew from a score to forty-five daily, and a hundred people were converted on the Sunday previous to the penning of the report. The enthusiastic correspondent stated:

"The work is taking within its range persons of all classes. Men of low degree, and men of high estate for wealth and position; old men and maidens, and even little children, are seen humbly kneeling together pleading for grace. The mayor of the city, with other persons of like position, are not ashamed to be seen bowed at the altar of prayer beside the humble servant..."

It is somewhat significant that Hamilton's "gust of Divine power" reportedly sweeping throughout the entire community "took its rise in the rise of the laity" and was entirely spontaneous. This rise to leadership on the part of the laymen became typical of the great movement that followed. Indeed, the Hamilton revival bore all the marks of the subsequent American revivals, save one, the union-prayer-meeting feature developed in New York City and popularized throughout the United States.

The account of this extraordinary revival of religion was read by hundreds of wistful pastors in the Methodist Episcopal Church, America's largest and most evangelistic body of believers at that time. The expectancy created by the Hamilton outbreak of early October was discussed in an article on the revival sweeping the nation, six months later. Spiritual awakenings are exceedingly infectious, and proximity in time and place adds to the stimulation of desire for similar blessing. The appearance of the account of the Hamilton revival in the *Christian Advocate* was followed by a steadily increasing number of paragraphs describing local revivals, few in number in November, increasing in December, and a veritable flood in the late winter and spring of 1858.

Among the signs of preparation of heart for an awakening was the calling of a convention at Pittsburgh on December 1, 1857. This was under Presbyterian auspices, and was largely attended by ministers from the Synods of Pittsburgh, Allegheny, Wheeling, and Ohio. The convention continued in session for three days, considering the necessity of a general revival of religion in all the churches represented and others as well. The agenda of the meetings included the means, the encouragements, the hindrances, the demand of the times, the indications of divine providence, and everything relating to this momentous question of revival. It was a solemn, anxious, melting and encouraging meeting. Two hundred ministers and many laymen attended, and much of the time was spent in prayer. A committee was appointed to draw up an address to the churches, to be read from the pulpits by the pastors. It was also recommended that the official members of the respective churches be called together to discuss the convention agenda, and, above all, that the people be called together to pray. As a result of this programme, multitudes of ministers of the Presbyterian and other faiths delivered messages on the first Sunday of the New Year (1858) on the subject of revival, and the first Thursday was observed as a day of humiliation, fasting and prayer. An intelligent and mighty impulse was felt. Shortly afterwards, another and similar convention was called at Cincinnati. The convention was a great prayer-meeting, and the churches participating were stirred.

On July 1, 1857, a quiet and zealous business-man named Jeremiah Lanphier took up an appointment as a City Missionary in downtown New York. He had been born in Coxsachie, New York, in 1809, and had been converted in 1842 in the Broadway Tabernacle built by Charles G. Finney a decade earlier. A local journalist described Lanphier as "tall, with a pleasant face, an affectionate manner, and indomitable energy and perseverance; a good singer, gifted in prayer and exhortation, a welcome guest to any house, shrewd and endowed with much tact and common sense."

It was the North Church of the Dutch Reformed faith that appointed Lanphier. This church was suffering from depletion of membership due to the removal of population from the downtown section to better residential quarters, and the new City Missionary was engaged to make diligent visitation in the immediate neighbourhood with a view to enlisting church attendance among the floating population of the lower city. The Dutch Consistory felt that it had appointed an ideal layman for the task in hand, and so it was.

Burdened by the need, Jeremiah Lanphier decided to invite others to join him in a noonday prayer-meeting, to be held once a week on Wednesdays. He therefore distributed a handbill:

"How Often Shall I Pray?

"As often as the language of prayer is in my heart; as often as I see my need of help; as often as I feel the power of temptation; as often as I am made sensible of any spiritual declension, or feel the aggression of a worldly, earthly spirit.

"In prayer we leave the business of time for that of eternity, and intercourse with men for intercourse with God.

•   •   •   •   •

"A day Prayer-Meeting is held every Wednesday, from 12 to 1 o'clock, in the Consistory building, in the rear of the North Dutch Church, corner of Fulton and William Streets (entrance from Fulton and Ann Streets).

"This meeting is intended to give merchants, mechanics, clerks, strangers, and business-men generally, an opportunity to stop and call upon God amid the perplexities incident to their respective avocations. It will continue for one hour; but it is also designed for those who may find it inconvenient to remain more than 5 or 10 minutes, as well as for those who can spare the whole hour."

Accordingly, at twelve noon, September 23, 1857, the door was opened and the faithful Lanphier took his seat to await the response to his invitation. Five minutes went by. No one appeared. The Missionary paced the room in a conflict of fear and faith. Ten minutes elapsed. Still no one came. Fifteen minutes passed. Lanphier was yet alone. Twenty minutes; twenty-five; thirty; and then at 12.30 p.m., a step was heard on the stairs, and the first person appeared, then another, and another, and another, until six people were present and the prayer-meeting began. On the following Wednesday, the six had become twenty, and on the third Wednesday, October 7, there were forty intercessors.

Thus, in the first week of October, 1857, it was decided to hold the meeting daily instead of weekly. In the same week, extraordinary revival of religion swept the city of Hamilton in faraway Canada. In the second week of October, the great financial panic of that year reached a crisis and prostrated business everywhere.

It is impossible not to connect the three events, for in them was demonstrated the need of religious revival, the means by which to accomplish it, and the provision of Divine grace to meet the situation.

Within six months, ten thousand business-men were gathering daily for prayer in New York, and within two years, a million converts had been added to the American churches. The Fulton Street Prayer Meeting continued daily (excepting holidays) to this present generation.

CHAPTER TWO

THE RISING TIDE

A T THE turn of the New Year 1858, the city of New York had a population of eight hundred thousand people, including neither the inhabitants of Brooklyn nor of the other Boroughs now in New York. New York was by no means an irreligious city, for there were church sittings for fully one-quarter of the inhabitants, and church attendance was fairly good. Unlike the New York of the twentieth century, it was a predominantly evangelical Protestant city. There were fifty Protestant Episcopal churches, forty-one Presbyterian, thirty-four Methodist Episcopal, twenty-nine Baptist, twenty-three Dutch Reformed, seven Congregationalist, seven Lutheran, five Reformed Presbyterian, four Associate Presbyterian, and eighty other churches.

Notices of revivals of religion began to appear in the religious press at the beginning of the year. Meanwhile, the faithful Fulton Street meeting was ever growing in strength, and prayers were being answered in the droppings and the showers of blessing. The Gothic Church in Brooklyn reported seventy-five conversions in a local revival in January. During the same month, a thorough revival swept the Hudson River town of Yonkers, when nearly ninety conversions occurred. Over in New Jersey territory, unusual awakenings were beginning, and across the whole country was increasing an expectancy of a downpour of Divine blessing. As yet, the revival was in its preparatory stage, with the quickening quite obvious to the ministers of the various churches but unnoticed by the general public and secular press.

In the month of February, showers of blessing had increased so much that they had become a deluge of no mean proportions. The secular press, noticing that something unprecedented was happening, began to give space to the news of the revival. On February 10, 1858, the New York *Daily Tribune* gave the movement widespread publicity in an editorial.

"The Hour of Prayer

"Some two or three years ago, a daily prayer-meeting was started in the lower portion of the city, which met from 12 to 1 o'clock p.m. with a view to giving merchants and merchants' clerks an opportunity of uniting in acknowledgment of their obligations to Divine grace and mercy. A few months ago, after a long silence, this meeting was revived at the Consistory of the North Dutch Church at the corner of Fulton and William Streets, and has been crowded every day since the commencement of the financial panic.

"Another meeting has been established up town in the Ninth Street Dutch Reformed Church and was opened yesterday at noon. Upwards of two hundred persons were present including several clergymen, and great interest prevailed.

"We understand that arrangements are being made for the establishment of one or two additional meetings in the upper portion of the city, and soon the striking of the five bells at 12 o'clock will be generally known as the signal for the 'Hour of Prayer'. These meetings are non-denominational. The advancement of sectarian views is not tolerated in any form."

Two weeks later, the same journal announced that Religious Inquiry Meetings had been begun every day in the Norfolk Street Church, of which Dr. Armitage was the pastor. The hour was from 4 till 6 p.m., and the attendance was already noteworthy. The same journal reported that the Ninth Street Noonday Prayer Meeting had overflowed. Another Noonday meeting was begun in the Methodist Episcopal Church in Forsythe Street.

Meanwhile, Fulton Street, the original meeting place, was trying to accommodate crowds by holding three simultaneous prayer meetings one above the other in rooms in the same building. The seats were all filled, and the passages were so crowded that it was scarcely possible for people to pass in or out. Hundreds were unable to gain admission, and a demand arose for more meetings at noon. It was not surprising to note another item in the press:

"A businessmen's union prayer-meeting is held daily from 12 to 1 o'clock in the John Street Methodist Church, number 44 John Street, a few doors east of Broadway. This meeting is similar to the one held in Fulton Street. Owing to the overcrowded state of the rooms in that place and the manifest increasing interest, it has been thought best to open this place also."

Undoubtedly the greatest revival in New York's colourful history was sweeping the city, and it was of such an order to make the whole nation curious. There was no fanaticism, no hysteria, just an incredible movement of the people to pray. The services were not given over to preaching. Instead, *anyone* was free to pray! *The National Intelligencer* in the capital, Washington, noted that in New York "a religious interest has been growing in the midst of the rowdyism everywhere so long prevalent." "Religious revivals were never more numerous or effective than at present."

The churches began to feel the impact of the noonday meetings, which were largely laymen's voluntary efforts. A typical example of the reaction in the churches may be seen in the fact that on March 14 (Sunday), the Thirteenth Presbyterian Church of New York City received 113 by profession of faith in Christ and 14 by letter. Of these professions, 26 were heads of families, 10 were Sunday School teachers, and 62 Sunday School folks. Of the total, 63 were between the ages of twelve and twenty, 50 over twenty, and 10 over forty years of age.

On March 17, Burton's Theatre in Chambers Street, was thrown open for noonday prayer-meetings. The meetings were initiated by merchants doing business in the neighbourhood of Chambers Street, and was continued by them at their own expense. Mr. Burton, the owner of the theatre, was perfectly willing for them to operate religious services there, and he himself expressed a desire to be prayed for. Half an hour before the time appointed for the service, the theatre was packed in every corner from the pit to the roof. By noon, the entrances were so thronged that it required great exertions to get within hearing distance, and no amount of elbowing could force an entrance so far as to gain a sight of the stage! People clung to every projection along the walls, and they piled themselves upon the seats and crowded the stage beneath, above and behind the curtain. The street in front was crowded with vehicles, and the excitement was tremendous. Nearly all the assembly were businessmen, only two hundred being ladies and fifty clergymen. Rev. Theodore Cuyler led the services that day.

Three days later, the *New York Times* reported that Dr. Henry Ward Beecher led three thousand people in devotions in Burton's Theatre. During his remarks, he was interrupted by singing from an overflow meeting in the Bar-room, whereupon he led the vast throng in thanksgiving that such a thing could take place. A couple of days later, the *Herald* stated in a column titled "The Revivals" that Chauncey Schaffer had led a two-hour meeting in the same theatre.

A two-column write-up on the front page gave a significant review of the movement in New York City, establishing that in New York City (Manhattan without Brooklyn) at least 6,110 people were in attendance at daily prayer-meetings. Here is a bird's-eye view of the situation on March 26:

Fulton Street	(Dutch Reformed)	300
John Street	(Methodist Episcopal)	600
Burton's Theatre	(Union)	1,200
Ninth Street	(Dutch Reformed)	150
Church of the Puritans	(Congregationalists)	125
Broome Street	(Dutch Reformed)	300
Waverley Place	(Y.M.C.A.)	200
Mercer Street	(Union)	150
Madison Square	(Presbyterian)	200
Trinity 34th Street	(Methodist Episcopal)	250

Another dozen places were in the list, which was still incomplete.

The most sensational conversion in March was that of Orville Gardner, a pugilist better known as "awful" Gardner. Gardner's public testimony had a widespread effect on a certain class of citizens. Before very long ten thousand New Yorkers had been converted to God and were in the care of the churches, and in May a good authority gave the total for the City as fifty thousand converts. The American press from coast to coast carried news of the great awakening in the metropolis, and citizens everywhere were challenged by the movement. The showers of blessing had caused a flood in New York, and this flood suddenly burst its bounds and swept over New England, engulfed the Ohio Valley cities and states, rolled over the newly settled West, lapped the edges of the mountains in the South, and covered the United States of America and Canada with Divine favour.

The most publicized work of grace was undoubtedly the condition prevailing in the metropolis of New York, but the phenomenon of packed churches and startling conversions was noted everywhere.

There seemed to be three streams of blessing flowing out from the Middle Atlantic States, one northwards to New England, another southwards as far as Texas, and a third westwards along the Ohio valley. An observer in a leading secular newspaper stated it well when he wrote: "The Revivals, or Great Awakening, continue to be the leading topic of the day... from Texas, in the South, to the extreme of our Western boundaries and our Eastern limits; their influence is felt by every denomination." Newspapers from Maine to Louisiana reflected his view.

As early as the beginning of February, "extensive revivals... now prevailing in the Methodist Episcopal Church all over the country" were reported to the denomination's leading journal, which observed that its exchanges with its Methodist contemporaries in the Central, Pittsburgh, Northwestern, Western, and its own territories, told of a total of eight thousand people converted in Methodist meetings in one week.

A Baptist journal attempted to keep abreast of the news of conversions reaching its offices, but its editor apparently gave up the task after listing seventeen thousand conversions reported to him by Baptist leaders in three weeks. These figures are exceedingly incomplete, and have only an impressional value. They were reported as follows:

Maine	411	Ohio	1148
New Hampshire	82	Indiana	737
Vermont	304	Illinois	1146
Massachusetts	2575	Michigan	604
Rhode Island	387	Wisconsin	465
Connecticut	795	Iowa	278
New York	2386	Minnesota	388
Pennsylvania	1746	Missouri	424
New Jersey	698	Tennessee	711
Delaware	40	Virginia	205
Maryland	9	Other States	177
District of Columbia	21	Canada	287

It should be noted that these figures are simply those which were reported to the editor concerned, and do not represent the actual conditions in any state, although it is probable that the details for states close to New York are more accurate than those farther away.

There was another attempt at estimating the actual number of converts, again "exceedingly incomplete" and valuable only for the relative proportions in various states. It gives the figures available in May, 1858:

Maine	2670	Missouri	2,027
New Hampshire	1376	Kentucky	2,666
Vermont	770	Tennessee	1,666

Massachusetts	6254	District of Columbia	93
Rhode Island	1,331	Delaware	179
Connecticut	2,799	Maryland	1,806
New York	16,674	Virginia	1,005
New Jersey	6,035	North Carolina	558
Pennsylvania	6,732	South Carolina	127
Ohio	8,009	Georgia	250
Illinois	10,460	Alabama	372
Indiana	4,775	Florida	25
Michigan	8,081	Mississippi	135
Wisconsin	1,467	Texas	27
Iowa	2,179	California	50
Minnesota	508		

Again it should be noted that these represent figures, from all denominations, that happened to be available to a New York editor. The total of 96,216 people converted to God in a few months is nevertheless heartening.

The influence of the awakening was felt everywhere in the nation. It first moved the great cities, but it also spread through every town and village and country hamlet. It swamped schools and colleges. It affected all classes without respect to condition. A Divine influence seemed to pervade the land, and men's hearts were strangely warmed by a Power that was outpoured in unusual ways. There was no fanaticism. There was remarkable unanimity of approval among religious and secular observers alike, with scarcely a critical voice heard anywhere. It seemed to many that the fruits of Pentecost had been repeated a thousandfold. At any rate, the number of conversions reported soon reached the total of fifty thousand weekly, a figure borne out by the fact that church statistics show an average of ten thousand additions to church membership weekly for the period of two years.

CHAPTER THREE

NEW ENGLAND TO NEW ORLEANS

THROUGHOUT the 'fifties, church attendance in New England had remained high, with fully one-quarter of the population attending church regularly, another quarter occasionally. But New England was always a fruitful ground for theological controversy, producing the most rigid conservatives and the most volatile radicals in America. Finney visited the city of Boston in the winter of 1856, and found that his vital religion was opposed strongly by some very orthodox theologians. Boston was the happy hunting ground of controversialists, and a divisive spirit was prevalent in the churches.

A daily prayer-meeting had been held in Boston for several years before the 1858 Awakening. Interest in a religious revival continued to increase, and it was decided to commence a businessmen's prayer meeting in the Old South Church, which was convenient to the business centre of the city. To the surprise of the sponsor, a businessman, the place was crowded the first day, and multitudes could not get in at all.

Early in March 1858, the secular press began to take notice of the revival, declaring that religious excitement was on the increase. Finney, all the while, was holding forth in Park Street Church, preaching on such evangelistic topics as "Being Found in Christ" and "Instructions to Inquirers". By that time, the revival had swept throughout the city, and had become (to quote Finney) "too general to keep any account at all of the number of converts, or to allow of any estimate being made that would approximate the truth".

By the middle of March, the awakening in Boston, like its counterpart in New York City, became news to the whole nation. The Boston correspondent of a Washington paper wrote his editor that the chief concern in many cities and towns of New England was *religion*.

The meetings (he declared) were usually crowded and solemn, with the whole assembly sometimes in tears under the melting power of the Holy Spirit. A few days later, the same journal reported that amongst other instances it was stated "that there are several New England towns in which not a single adult person can be found unconverted", a report which appeared in various publications, secular and religious.

Typical of the prayer-meetings in Boston is another notice.

"On account of the crowd that daily throngs Father Mason's chapel in North Street, unable to gain admittance, Father Taylor has thrown open the Bethel in North Square, and a Prayer-Meeting will be held daily in that place from 12 to 1 o'clock."

Professor Finney reported that the daily prayer-meeting in Park Street Church filled the church on every occasion announced: while Mrs. Finney held a Ladies' Prayer-Meeting in the large vestry of the church, which became so crowded that the good women stood outside wherever it was possible to hear the proceedings. South Baptist Church held a daily meeting from 8 a.m. till 9 a.m. The Old South Chapel organized two: from 8.30 a.m.

till 9.30 and from noon till 1 p.m. Salem Street Church also had a meeting at noon, while Park Street Church and Church Street Methodist both held meetings daily at 3 p.m. Tremont Temple had its daily prayer-meeting from 4 p.m. until 5 p.m., and the Y.M.C.A. from 5.30 p.m. until 6.30 p.m. Most of the churches had evening meetings for pure evangelism. It is not surprising that Boston's 177,000 citizens seemed to be moved throughout. All classes were making inquiry everywhere, including large numbers of Unitarians, some of whose pastors organized daily prayer meetings.

The movement in New England generally was even stronger than in its metropolis. The largest denomination reported 11,744 additions on profession in the revival period, and another claimed 8,479 in a few months, while two hundred and sixty smaller centres of population reported over ten thousand conversions in a couple of months. In Springfield, Massachusetts, inquiry meetings were held by nearly every pastor in the city. In New Bedford, one in twenty of the population professed decision within a few months, and similar stirring awakenings were noted in Lynn and Haverhill. In the revival at Holliston, two hundred and fifty conversions occurred, a like number of additions being registered at Winchester. Unprecedented awakenings broke out at Lowell and Williamstown, and Orange, "a stronghold of error", was transformed by the movement. In Massachusetts, a total of one hundred and fifty towns were moved by the revival of religion, with five thousand conversions before the end of March.

Morning, noon, afternoon, and evening meetings were attended by great crowds in Portland, Maine, where the church bells daily summoned thousands to prayer. An extensive revival broke out in Bangor and the neighbouring towns; and in Biddeford, the movement was distinguished for the remarkable rapidity of the work of conversion, adults and heads of families being the outstanding fruit of the revival. Large accessions were made to the churches of Saco, and one hundred and ten persons were converted at Deer Isle.

The city of Providence, in Rhode Island, reported a time of religious interest never before known. Nearly every church was awakened and conversions became numerous. Morning prayer-meetings overflowed, and other meetings were fully attended, making a strong impression. It was noteworthy that there was no unhealthy excitement. At Pawtucket, the revival increased until over one hundred people were professedly born again. At Warren, a single Baptist church experienced a wave of blessing that resulted in the conversion of more than one hundred people. Another thirty-six towns reported a thousand decisions to accept Christ as Saviour.

In the State of Connecticut, the revival swept the communities in an unprecedented way. One of the largest churches in New Haven was crowded to excess for an 8 a.m. prayer meeting, repeating the daily achievement at 5 p.m. Equally large prayer-meetings were launched in Hartford and New London. At Bethel, business was suspended for an hour every day between the hours of 4 and 5 p.m., and two hundred persons were reported converted in two months, three-quarters of whom joined the Congregational Church. Connecticut also reported a town where no unconverted adult could be found.

In the neighbouring states of Vermont and New Hampshire, revivals broke out in Dartmouth College, Brattleboro, Claremont, Northfield, St. Alban's, Burlington, Castleton, Middlesbury, Derby and Manchester, in all of which daily prayer-meetings were launched with success. Two hundred conversions were reported from Dover and New Ipswich, and forty other New Hampshire towns reported four hundred and twenty-five additions, while forty Vermont towns reported over six hundred conversions. In Rutland, Vermont, two hundred people were led to decision for Christ, seventy in a single meeting.

Outstanding in the results of the revival in New England was the work among the Colleges. Yale experienced an awakening in which it was "impossible to estimate the conversions", and Amherst's President reported that nearly all the students there had been converted. Professors of an experience of religion were given as forty-five seniors, sixty-two juniors, sixty sophomores, and thirty-seven freshmen at Yale. Such is a fleeting glimpse of the revival in New England, 1857-8.

The State of New York was soon swept by a wave of religious interest comparable to the one being experienced in its greatest centre of population. Along the beautiful Hudson River, busy little towns and cities witnessed unusual happenings. At Hudson, the Dutch Reformed, Baptist, Methodist, and Presbyterian churches launched a daily prayer meeting as a union effort, the people coming "as doves to their windows" to throng the place beyond precedent. At Yonkers, more than two hundred people were converted in a few weeks. The Washington Street Methodist Episcopal Church in Poughkeepsie, where meetings were held every day, found its altar-rails crowded with inquirers, and in three weeks of special meetings in all the churches, three hundred people sought salvation. Peekskill, a reputedly wicked town, saw the same means used and the same results achieved. At Kingston, Ulster County, the union prayer-meetings overflowed from one church to another. Farther up the river at Troy, merchants, clerks and professional men particularly showed an interest in their own spiritual welfare, and meetings were held daily and nightly in the churches, which gained several hundred additions. Catskill, formerly sunken in religious indifference, saw a revival commence through the conversion of a young Bible-class attender; every other member became converted and 115 new members were soon afterwards received into church memberships. Albany, capital city with 60,000 population, was the scene of unusual happenings. An early morning prayer-meeting was initiated by State Legislators, who began with six participants in the rooms of the Court of Appeals opposite the Senate Chamber; soon afterwards the rooms were overflowing. Regular noon prayer-meetings attracted great crowds in Albany, as elsewhere. The Baptist pastor in Union Village baptized 111 converts and expected to baptize more, saying that he had never witnessed a revival of such extent where there was manifest so little mere sympathetic excitement. More than fifty of those baptized were heads of families between the ages of 25 and 50, one being a man in his eighty-third year. One hundred and forty people decided in Olean; two hundred in Cold Spring.

Typical of the revivals in New York State's smaller cities is a report from Salem, which said:

"Without any alarming event, without any extraordinary preaching or any special effort or other means that might be supposed peculiarly adapted to interest the minds of the people, there has within a short time past been, in several towns and villages in Washington and Warren Counties, and towns and villages along the western parts of the State of Vermont, a revival so extraordinary as to attract the attention of all classes of the community. In one town, over a hundred have been brought to conviction and conversion, and the glorious work is still going on; they expect the whole town will be converted—for this they pray. This work does not appear to be confined to the churches; hundreds are converted at prayer-meetings, in private homes, in the workshops, and at their work in the fields. Men of fortune and fashion, lawyers, physicians, and tradesmen and indeed all classes, ages, and sexes, are the subjects of it."

Further west, along the strategic Mohawk River, similar revivals broke out in the towns and villages. In Schenectady, church bells sounded every evening, calling great crowds to meeting, filling every church. Two popular prayer-meetings held daily bore much fruit, and converts came into church fellowship with surprising rapidity. The ice on the Mohawk was broken for believers' baptism. From the month of December onwards in Utica, the pastors of the evangelical churches united in union prayer-meetings held in rotation in the various churches; the movement was so well supported that the early morning prayer service in a large church was filled with worshippers, some frequently having to stand. Syracuse held its union service in Convention Hall. Geneva produced a revival of great stillness and solemnity, with numerous conversions and the usual prayer-meetings, one church trebling its membership. Buffalo witnessed a powerful revival of religion. Examples could be multiplied, for two hundred towns reported six thousand specific cases of conversion.

One of the first sections of the country to experience an awakening was the New Jersey area, which reported stirring revivals of religion as early as late October 1857. In Readington and Pennington, one hundred and twenty conversions occurred before the New Year, while blessing began in Newark in January with sixty additions in the Mount Lebanon Circuit. Orange Methodists rejoiced in no less than one hundred and twenty-five decisions in early February. Locality after locality experienced a revival of religious interest.

In the month of March, the awakening in New Jersey equalled anything on the American continent. The city of Newark, with a population of 70,000, witnessed startling evidences of the sweeping movement there. In a couple of months, 2,785 people professed conversion, averaging one hundred conversions in each reporting congregation. It became a common sight to see business-houses closed, with a notice "will reopen at the close of the prayer-meeting" and the union meetings thus advertised were crowded to overflowing. Extra efforts were made to reach members of the Fire Department with the gospel, and on one occasion, nearly two thousand firemen attended one such meeting at the National Hotel in Market Street. Dr. Scott, a leading Newark pastor, testified that the revival was winning the most mature minds in the community, saying that, in his opinion, the most mature personalities in his congregation were the forty-five who had just united with it by profession of faith in Christ.

Similar scenes of revival were witnessed in Paterson, New Jersey, where a successful union meeting was launched, as well as evening meetings, and all the churches reported accessions to membership. In Jersey City, large numbers professed conversions, and there a union meeting was held daily between 7 and 9 a.m. in the Lyceum on Grand Street. In New Brunswick, New Jersey, 177 joined the Methodist church, 112 of whom were heads of families, including steamboat captains and pilots, and in Trenton, the Methodists alone gained upwards of 1,700 additions. Sixty centres of revival in New Jersey reported approximately six thousand conversions.

Among the first attenders of the original Businessmen's Prayer- Meeting in New York City was a young man, not yet twenty-one years of age, hailing from Philadelphia. Upon his return to his home, he and some of his fellow Y.M.C.A. members approached the trustees of the Methodist Episcopal Church on Fourth Street below Arch Street, requesting the use of their lecture room for a similar meeting. The request was speedily granted, and the first noon prayer-meeting in Philadelphia was held in the Union Methodist Episcopal Church on November 23, 1857.

For a long time, however, the response of Philadelphia's businessmen was disappointing, for the average attendance was about a dozen people. But on February 3, 1858, the meeting was removed to a little ante-room in the spacious public hall owned by Dr. Jayne, popularly known as Jayne's Hall. Throughout February, the increase in attendance was gradual; twenty, thirty, forty, fifty and then sixty attending. The wave of revival reached the place in March.

At first only the small room was occupied, with a few in attendance. Then it became overflowing, and the meeting removed to the main saloon, starting meetings there on March 10. Twenty-five hundred seats were provided, and were filled to overflowing. The sponsors next removed a partition from the main floor space and platform; next the floor, platform and lower gallery; then the floor, platform, and both galleries; soon every nook and cranny in the place was full of worshipping people, and fully six thousand gathered daily at noontime for prayer.

In order to continue the work, which (as in New York) was flooding the churches with inquirers and converts, a big canvas tent was bought for $2,000 and opened for religious services on May 1, 1858. During the following four months, an aggregate of 150,000 people attended the ministry under canvas, and many conversions resulted therefrom. The churches in Philadelphia were thoroughly aroused, and a sweeping revival continued all summer long.

Sixty-five other towns in Pennsylvania reported revivals of religion with five thousand conversions resulting. It is impossible to keep record of all the villages and country places that reported blessing, for even the most enthusiastic editors wearied of the task. In Pittsburgh, two daily prayer-meetings were launched to accommodate intercessors desiring to pray between the hours of 11.30 and 12.30 noon, about a thousand attending in these two places, and many more in meetings elsewhere in the city. The churches of Pittsburgh reaped a harvest of additions from the movement.

In Maryland, the revival really began in December, when there were sixty conversions reported from Havre de Grace, and over one hundred from the Monroe Circuit of Baltimore Conference, both instances among Methodists. In the spring, daily prayer-meetings were launched by the Y.M.C.A. with encouraging attendances. Methodist journals continued to report great numbers of conversions from all around the State, and other denominations shared equally in the stirring.

At the nation's capital, five daily prayer-meetings were launched, commencing at 6.30 a.m., the Y.M.C.A. and the churches sponsoring the efforts. The *National*

Intelligencer described the meetings as "still and solemn", and on April 1 commented editorially that the religious excitement in the city was unabated, five thousand attending the prayer service in the Academy of Music Hall.

Writing of the Revival of 1858, no less a person than Charles G. Finney stated:

"Slavery seemed to shut it out from the South. The people there were in such a state of irritation, of vexation, and of committal to their peculiar institution, which had come to be assailed on every side, that the Spirit of God seemed to be grieved away from them. There seemed to be no place found for Him in the hearts of Southern people at that time."

Beardsley, a more recent historian, echoes Finney's sentiments, also held by many Northern historians. Both declaration and explanation became insecure in the light of research.

Bishop Candler, on the other hand, insists that the results of the revival were "in proportion to the population, greater in the South than in any other section", and his good account of the amazing revivals of religion in the Confederate Armies in the War between the States seem to give the lie to the contention that pro-slavery sentiment hindered revival in the South.

The *Southern Presbyterian Review*, July 1859, countered the Northern claim strongly, saying then "it is not Northern, nor Southern, Eastern nor Western" and declaring that the revival in the South had reached as far as the Florida reefs. There is good reason to believe that the revivals were as widespread in the South as the Northern States. Allowance should be made for the fact that the South possessed no great industrial cities like the Northern metropolitan areas, and that her population was scattered over an agricultural countryside; hence, it was less spectacular down South, where the newspapers could not immediately influence the crowded cities as up North.

A Northern authority testified, nevertheless, that revivals of more or less power were sweeping Wilmington, Baltimore, Washington, Richmond, Charleston, Nashville, Memphis, New Orleans, Mobile, Savannah, Augusta, Columbia and Raleigh. In Richmond, Virginia, a daily prayer-meeting was launched with success. In Lynchburg, in the same state, a revival of no mean dimensions converted many young men to the Christian faith. In Mobile, Alabama, sermons were preached daily in the Catholic, Episcopal, Baptist, and Methodist churches, with "unusually numerous converts". In April, when the secular press reported that the revival was declining in New York City, it assured its readers that the awakening was increasing in the Southern and Western States, where revivals had broken out in Nashville, Mobile, New Orleans, and Charleston, and was "by no means confined to the cities" of the Southland.

With these facts in mind, it is quite easy to believe that the revival swept the South in spite of the slavery issue. Bishop Candler quotes official statistics to show that in the years 1858, 1859, and 1860, over one hundred thousand converts were added to the Methodist Episcopal Church South, adding that the equally large Baptist denomination shared similar blessing. That being so, the revival in the South produced almost as many converts proportionately as the Northern States recorded.

CHAPTER FOUR

WEST OF THE ALLEGHANIES

EARLY in the year 1858, the wave of revival interest passed over the crest of the Appalachian system of mountains, and poured down the Ohio River Valley following the line of settlement established since pioneer days. Within two months, four-hundred-and-eighty towns had reported fifteen thousand conversions. The *Presbyterian Magazine* hastened to announce that the entire western country was sharing in the revival movement, adding the details that great revivals had broken out in Cincinnati, Louisville, Cleveland, Detroit, Indianapolis, Chicago, St. Louis, and Dubuque, and that the cities, villages, and country places of Ohio, Kentucky, Indiana, Michigan, Illinois, Missouri, Iowa, and Wisconsin were receiving revival increase. The *Western Christian Advocate*, exulting in the spiritual winning of the West, described awakenings in Ohio, Illinois, and Indiana; stating that forty-two Methodist Episcopal clergy reported 4,384 conversions in three months, 750 being in one place.

In Wheeling, Virginia (afterwards in West Virginia and properly belonging to the Ohio Valley system rather than to the South), it was reported that the past winter (1857-8) would long be remembered on account of the revivals of religion. Methodist leaders declared that there had been nothing to equal the strength of the movement, not even the glorious days of 1839-40 when the Methodist Episcopal Church received 154,000 additions. In some neighbourhoods of West Virginia, almost the entire adult population had been brought under the influence of the awakening, many churches reporting one hundred to two hundred accessions.

On the south bank of the Ohio River, Kentucky received an unprecedented stirring of religious interest. As in other cities further east, the newspapers in Louisville began to give space to revival intelligence in March, 1858. The Louisville *Daily Courier* of March 6 noticed that the Brook Street Methodist Episcopal Church had received about a hundred new members, three-quarters of them by profession of new-found faith in Christ. Within a week, the revival had become the talk of the town, for the same journal announced that the churches of Louisville were open day and night caring for souls.

Union prayer-meetings were soon launched in Kentucky's big city, secular journalists observing that the meetings were growing in such interest that it was impossible for the Y.M.C.A. premises to accommodate the crowds, hence a move to the large Masonic Temple was contemplated, meetings to be held daily at 7.45 a.m., lasting until 9 a.m. The *Daily Courier* of March 27 announced in a column headed *The Religious Awakening* that long before the appointed hour of the meeting, the large hall of the Masonic Temple was filled to overflowing, more than a thousand eager people being in attendance. The meeting began with

"Amazing Grace, how sweet the sound
That saved a wretch like me!
Once I was lost, but now am found,
Was blind, but now I see."

The exuberance and concern of the meeting infected the secular journalists. One would think that the press had been converted.

Two days later, the same journal declared that the meeting of the previous day had broken all records, the largest crowd yet seen there being unable to find space in the Masonic Temple. Meanwhile, daily prayer-meetings were increasing, their influence pervading the city, and over a thousand conversions resulting to the praise of God. *The Religious Movement* claimed a column in further issues of the newspaper, the last issue of March observing that the Masonic Temple had again been packed, while other prayer-meetings had grown in catering for the overflowing crowds of praying people. In early April, four popular prayer-meetings attracted crowds to the Masonic Temple, the Mechanic's Library, the Key Engine House, and the Relief Engine House. A reporter, on April 5, said that an "immense concourse" had entirely filled the Masonic Temple at an early hour, necessitating the holding of an overflow meeting. Next day, an editorial declared that there was no abatement of interest and no diminution of attendance, observing that licentiousness had been restrained and that "drunkard-manufacturers" had become apprehensive of their trade prospects. Other prayer-meetings grew and abounded, one being launched in the Lafayette Engine House.

By April 8, such had been the improvement in the city's morals and such were the reports from the rest of Kentucky and the other States, that it was thought by the press that the millennium had arrived at last. One writer stated his impressions thus:

"The Spirit of God seems to be brooding over our city, and to have produced an unusual degree of tenderness and solemnity in all classes. Never since our residence in the city have we seen so fair a prospect for a general and thorough work of grace as is now indicated."

Revival had already broken out in Lexington, Covington, Frankfort, and other towns throughout the entire state.

The Ohio River figured in two items of revival news. Under the heading *Add Colour to Revival*, it was announced that eighteen coloured converts of the revival had been baptized in the river. And the *Daily Courier* was informed that on the steamer *Telegraph* of the Cincinnati and Louisville Mail Packet Line, the religious revival was the universal topic on the voyage up river, a prayer-meeting having been held in the Main Saloon until a late hour.

Across the river, in the State of Ohio, two hundred towns reported twelve thousand conversions in a couple of months. In Cincinnati, the attendance at the daily prayer-meetings became so large that the venue chosen was unable to accommodate the crowds, necessitating a move to the large First Presbyterian Church. The Cincinnati *Daily Commercial* commented (April 2, 1858) that "Religious excitement in the city is unabated, and the churches are becoming more popular every day with citizens unaccustomed to modes of grace." In the city of Cleveland, population forty thousand, the united attendance at the early morning prayer-meetings throughout the city churches was about two thousand. The whole community was stirred. The Plymouth Congregational Church held five meetings daily from six in the morning until nine at night. A thousand people were received into fellowships in a couple of months. The Methodist Episcopal Church of Circleville, Ohio, received two hundred and ten accessions, with others promised, while the other churches in the same town were receiving thirties and forties.

In Indiana, one hundred and fifty towns reported from four to five thousand conversions in two months of revival. Noon-day prayer-meetings were launched in Indianapolis, the State capital, and religious interest pervaded the town. At Detroit, Michigan, morning prayer-meetings held in the downtown Baptist and Congregationalist churches, were crowded by businessmen of all denominations. Congress Street Methodist Church reported over one hundred and forty conversions, and numerous inquirers and decisions were reported in all the other churches. Six Michigan towns reported religious revivals with between fifteen hundred and two thousand conversions recorded.

There was a striking instance of the power of prayer demonstrated in Kalamazzo, in Michigan. There the Episcopalians, Baptists, Methodists, Presbyterians, and Congregationalists united in announcing a prayer-meeting. The ecumenical effort was launched in fear and trembling, it being wondered if the public would consider attending a prayer-meeting.

At the very first meeting a request was read: "A praying wife requests the prayers of this meeting for her unconverted husband." All at once a burly man arose and said: "I am that man. I have a praying wife, and this request must be for me. I want you to pray for me!"

As soon as he was seated, another man, seemingly ignoring his predecessor, arose in sobs and tears to say:

"I am that man. I have a praying wife. She prays for me. And now she asks *you* to pray for me. I am sure I am that man, and I want you to pray for me!"

Five other convicted husbands requested prayer, and

the power of God fell upon the assembly. Before long, there were between four and five hundred conversions in the town.

Farther west, an unusual interest manifested itself in St. Louis, Missouri, both in the churches and in the business circles of the city. The union prayer-meetings were well attended by all classes of people, among whom great seriousness existed: and all the churches were crowded. In St. Joseph, a great revival broke out, the churches of the city uniting to carry on the work. Whole families were converted. Similar blessing was reported from St. Charles. The Rev. J. B. Fuller, nephew of England's famous Andrew Fuller, produced great excitement in Missouri by his preaching, being a converted actor and only seventeen years old. Fifty revival centres in Missouri reported two thousand conversions, while three times that number in Illinois announced between three and four thousand conversions. A thousand converts found salvation in Wisconsin in the early part of 1858, and about the same number was reported from Minnesota Territory. Three hundred accessions were made by the Minneapolis churches, and a private correspondent, in St. Paul, wrote that "the good work of the Lord goes on. The interest is still on the increase. St. Paul never saw a time like the present. The Holy Spirit seems to pervade the entire community, in every department of business". The *Congregational Herald* observed that never before had such a general interest in religion existed in Dubuque, Iowa; and sixty other towns sharing in the revival reported fifteen hundred conversions. And far across the deserts and mountains, revival broke out in California.

In the autumn of 1856, a young man named Dwight Lyman Moody arrived in the budding metropolis of

Chicago. The events of the next two years, as they transpired in the Illinois city, were destined to shape his life in a way that has received scant treatment at the hands of all his biographers.

Chicago, built upon a mud-flat on the shores of Lake Michigan, had only thirty thousand inhabitants in 1850; but in 1860 it could boast of more than one hundred thousand citizens. It was a booming city, but it was also a wicked place, combining as it does today a reputation for crime with a renown for aggressive Christian work.

Chicago was hit by the depression of 1857, but not as badly as were eastern cities, for it was enjoying a local boom due to the opening-up of the Middle West. There were a few signs of revival in 1857, but the turn of the year brought interesting news. "There is a very interesting revival of religion in progress at the Wabash Avenue Methodist Episcopal Church, where meetings are held every evening, commencing at 7 o'clock. Seats free."

After that, there was little mention of local revivals for the first two months of the New Year, but by the month of March the state of religion had become a phenomenon. Two hundred people had already been converted in four Methodist churches, Desplaines Street Church leading with sixty converts, followed by Wabash Avenue Church with fifty or more. Over a hundred had been converted in First, Second, Third, and Olivet Presbyterian Churches, where 8 a.m. prayer-meetings were in full swing daily. Trinity Episcopal Church had a noonday prayer-meeting, and the Dutch Reformed Church reported marked interest. First Baptist Church noted an increase, and in Tabernacle (afterwards Second) Baptist Church there had been fifty conversions in meetings which had been begun before the New Year. In many cases, the proportion of heads of families converted was noticeably high, up to fifty per cent of the converts.

On March 13, the Chicago *Daily Press* carried a full column of religious news, entitled "The Religious Awakening".

"A large class of our readers, we are assured, will be interested in such details as we have been able to collect in a form meeting our purpose, of the extent to which Chicago has shared in the general religious awakening that has been one of the most marked events of the year, throughout the entire country, East and West.

"In the larger cities of the East and in New York City especially, this movement, in the increased zeal of Christians and the awakening and conversion of those previously unconcerned and careless in religious matters, has become a prominent topic among the news of the day, so large a portion of those communities have been sharing in and yielding to the influences at work which has had steady, silent and solemn progress, without noise or excitement."

A review of the progress of the revival in individual churches followed, with the further editorial comment that

"in all these religious efforts there has been no appearance of excitement and no unusual means used; but the movement has been quiet, deep and effective. The pastors of the churches have had very little assistance. "

On March 19, a proposal was made to organize a general prayer-meeting of the union-type, similar to the New York and Philadelphia meetings. Within a week, the Press described it as "gaining strength daily" with upwards of twelve hundred persons present in the Metropolitan Hall, with the early morning prayer-meetings increasing all the while. On March 25, the newspapers, saying that it was so "unusual and almost unprecedented that the secular press should be called upon to refer beyond a brief notice to religious affairs in the community", reported that two thousand people now gathered daily at noontime for prayer in the Metropolitan Hall.

A letter from Chicago, dated March 21, described the situation:

"The religious interest now existing in this city is very remarkable. More than 2,000 businessmen meet at the noon prayer-meeting. The Metropolitan Hall is crowded to suffocation. The interest in the First Baptist Church is beyond anything ever known in this city, and exceeds anything I have ever seen in my life. Some who have come to the city on business, have become so distressed about their condition as sinners before God, that they have entirely forgotten their business in the earnestness of their desire for salvation. I am amazed to see such evidences of God's grace and power manifested among men. I might add that the First Baptist Church has daily meetings from eight to nine in the morning, twelve to one at noon, and six-and-a-half o'clock evening. The church today has had an all-day meeting."

At the end of that week, the Press reported that "nothing like the present general interest has ever occurred in the history of Chicago" and it commented on the perfect union of all evangelical Christians. A long column gave a religious review of the week, telling of morning and noontime meetings in a dozen churches of all denominations, with conversions daily. First Presbyterian

Church reported seventy-five enquirers; St. John's Episcopal told of nearly forty added, many anxiously enquiring the way of salvation; Union Park Baptist gave a week's increase as forty converts; and Tabernacle Baptist rejoiced in twenty-four conversions on the Lord's Day. The coloured community was also strongly affected by the revival, and conversions were reported by the Baptist of negro stock. And so the religious awakening swept everything before it during March 1858.

The coming of temptingly good weather in April brought about a slackening of attendance at the main meeting at Metropolitan Hall. Over a thousand people were still regular supporters of the prayer-meeting, but the curious and spurious had dropped off. The columns of the Chicago papers gave less space, but reported a continuance of interest as heretofore. By April 20, the noonday meeting at Metropolitan Hall (which had never attracted less than five hundred people) was transferred to the First Baptist Church. The revival began to run in different channels, there being an increase of evening meetings of an evangelistic nature, with a thousand conversions in all the churches to date. The revival continued in full swing during April. In May, it showed a new trend.

"The revival interest in the city is gradually retiring from the Union meetings into the individual churches. The number of prayer-meetings has increased, but not the attendance. About 1,800 attend in the daytime and 5,000 at night. Large numbers are constantly joining the churches, so constantly as to excite curiosity no longer."

Herewith, a typical example of this trend is seen in the item reported that Dr. Hatfield (Presbyterian) had received eighty-two persons on the previous Sabbath, more than half the number being heads of families. The church, which had had 177 members in 1856, now reported 508. Another item stated that a little boy of fifteen years and small of stature had been preaching to the Baptists with simple elegance, although (it was thought) a slight Irish accent marred his delivery. On May 24, the Moderator of the Presbyterian General Assembly (meeting that year in Chicago) declared that they were witnessing "scenes of revival such as the Church of Christ had never enjoyed as richly before".

The question naturally arises: How permanent were the results of the revival in Chicago? A generation later, Andreas published his heavy *History of Chicago*, and it is learned from Church records that the year 1858 was outstanding in the history of many Chicago churches. Union Park Baptist Church recorded great revivals in the winters of 1858 and 1859, in which considerable numbers were added to the membership. Trinity Episcopal, which had 152 members in 1855, 186 in 1856, 121 in 1857, built a new church to seat 1,400 in 1860. Third Baptist Church remembered a protracted meeting of three weeks beginning January 28, 1858, when the pastor (as evangelist) added twenty converts to the church. Second Presbyterian, after a lean year with the smallest number of converts in 1857 (only nineteen), recorded 1858 as of especial interest, there having been large numbers of converts exceeding 100 both among the adults and children of the congregation. First Presbyterian added about seventy-five on profession of faith in 1858 "in consequence of a powerful revival" which gave an impulse to the spiritual activities of the church. Alas, South Presbyterian Church reported only a limited number of additions, due to an unfortunate church quarrel about the property and about the slavery issue.

Other churches that engraved the revival in their congregational histories were the Church of the Atonement which had large additions to the membership in 1858, and the Plymouth Congregational, of which Moody was a member. It was during this winter and spring that Moody received his first great challenge to Christian work, writing to his mother in New England to tell of his constant attendance at services and his delight at the results therein. It was during the hot summer of 1858 that Moody got together a class that he decided to teach, their first sessions being held on a stranded log alongside Lake Michigan—such was the beginning of the world-famous Moody Memorial Church. The year 1858 was indeed a year of harvesting for Chicago Protestantism.

CHAPTER FIVE

THE AWAKENING IN ULSTER

THE connection between the people of the United States and those of the United Kingdom was always immediate, but most intimate was the connection between Ulster and the tens of thousands of Ulster Americans[1] in America. So it is not surprising that the General Assembly of the Presbyterian Church in Ireland sent an official deputation of two of its most honoured members to visit North America. Professor William Gibson, soon to be elected to the highest office in the Assembly, and Rev. William McClure visited the centres of revival in America, and the much-thrilled professor published his experiences in one city under the title *Pentecost, or the Work of God in Philadelphia.*

Throughout Ulster reports of the American Revival tended greatly to quicken the minds both of ministers and people. Many sermons on Revival were preached and prayer-meetings multiplied.

The first prayer-meeting appeared to be one begun in Kells near Ballymena by a young man named McQuilkin who had been reading the testimony of George Müller, the man of faith, as well as hearing of the Revival in America. James McQuilkin said to himself: "Why may we not have such a blessed work here, seeing that God did such things for Mr. Müller simply in answer to prayer?" Thus the

[1] Better known in America as the "Scotch-Irish"

Kells prayer-meeting became a Revival prayer-meeting.

James McQuilkin and his prayer helpers held a meeting on March 14, 1859, in the first Presbyterian Church in Ahoghill. Such large crowds attended that "it was deemed prudent to dismiss the meeting lest there be a fatal accident from the falling in of the galleries which threatened to give way under the alarming pressure". A layman thereupon addressed 3,000 people outside in the chilling rain, and, moved by his fervour and apostolic language, hundreds fell on their knees in the mud of the streets.

Three miles from Ahoghill is the prosperous market town of Ballymena, the hub of mid-Antrim, and nearby is the parish of Connor in which had begun the original prayer-meeting. At that time Ballymena had a population of 6,000, largely Presbyterian. The *Ballymena Observer* first noticed the Revival on March 26, 1859, and within six months had chronicled the events of the Awakening and its "extensive social, moral and religious improvements" already effected among the people.

Rev. Samuel J. Moore noted several cases of deep conviction among his charges. Upon his return from a meeting of the Presbyterian Synod, he found the town in a great state of excitement, many families having neglected their night's sleep for two preceding nights.

A group of prepared young laymen devoted almost their entire time to giving spiritual and physical comfort to the scores of people in need of it. Prayer-meetings were held at all hours of the day and night, and the evangelical churches were open for evening services, the Presbyterian, Episcopalian and Methodist ministers and people uniting in such efforts as well as in union prayer-meetings. Eye-witnesses added their descriptions of these extraordinary gatherings and results, such as one of about 5,000 people in a quarry.

In the month of May 1859 the Awakening made its appearance in Belfast, a town of 120,000 people, one third of whom were Roman Catholics. By the end of May the *Belfast News Letter* was giving a half-column or a column of space to Revival news. The outbreak of revival fervour in Belfast came through a visit of some of the "converts from Connor". It was in Berry Street Presbyterian Church that the greatest demonstration came. So many people lingered after the service that the Rev. Hugh Hanna reopened the church and took charge. On the Sunday following, most of the evangelical churches of the town were utterly overcrowded by interested people, and "the Revival" had full sway.

Dr. Knox, the bishop of the united dioceses of Down, Connor and Dromore, invited all his clergy to a breakfast in order to hear their opinion respecting the Revivals, which apparently had his careful support. All at length agreed that it was a work of God, but there was a difference of opinion among the clergy regarding the "prostrations" of sinners coming under conviction, some regarding them as hysteria, others as a Divine method of conviction. The Belfast Presbytery met and expressed its gratitude to God for the Revival, also urging caution regarding the physical manifestations. The ministers of the Wesleyan, Independent and Baptist churches supported the work from the start.

With something approaching unanimity, the ministers of Belfast launched a united prayer-meeting in the Music Hall, with the Mayor in the chair. The building was crowded to excess. A week later, the Bishop took the chair, assisted on the platform by the 146 clergymen, including the Moderator of the Presbyterian General Assembly, the President of the Wesleyan Methodist Conference, Presbyterian pastors and Episcopalian clergy, Baptists, Congregationalists, Methodists, and even the noted Dr. Montgomery of the Unitarian communion. Hundreds participated in overflow meetings, and thousands were turned away from this large building chosen for the meeting.

By June most of the evangelical churches were open and crowded for weekday services. Friends of the Revival estimated that 10,000 people were converted (only a small proportion of them violently by prostration) in the weeks and months which followed in Belfast. The Bishop declared in Trinity Church that he was satisfied that the Revival was doing much good.

Another development in the Belfast Revival came with the organizing of mass open-air meetings for prayer in the beautiful Botanic Gardens. At the end of June the first meeting attracted an assemblage never before seen in the north of Ireland. About 15,000 attended the first meeting over which the Presbyterian Moderator presided, and "results exceeded anything hitherto known" in Belfast.

In July the labours of ministers, visitors and converts in Belfast continued unabated in energy, zeal and success. The Rev. H. Grattan Guinness preached to at least 15,000 people in the open air. In August the churches of every denomination were crowded to excess, and visiting ministers from all over the three Kingdoms officiated in many pulpits. Another Botanic Gardens prayer-meeting on August 16, attracted 20,000, the proceedings being undertaken by the Y.M.C.A. In September the churches remained crowded, without any signs of weariness on the part of ministers or people, and in October the attendances were still "in no wise abated" although the novelty had worn off. The October meeting of the Maze Racecourse attracted 500 people instead of the customary 10,000. A large distillery, capable of turning out 1,000,000 gallons of whisky per annum, was put up by auction to be sold or to be dismantled. The Belfast reports were confirmed by the Evangelical Alliance meeting there.

Meanwhile the Ulster Revival began to spread into County Down. Writing from Holywood Palace, the Bishop notified Prof. Gibson that of 106 replies from clergy seventy-five gave gratifying testimony of the spiritual blessing.

The townsfolk of Coleraine, in the part of County Derry close to the County Antrim Revival centres, witnessed some of the most amazing scenes in the whole movement in Ireland. A schoolboy, under deep conviction of sin, seemed so incapable of continuing his studies that the kindly teacher sent him home in the company of another boy, already converted. On the way home the two boys noticed an empty house and entered it to pray. At last the unhappy boy found peace, and returned immediately to the classroom to tell his teacher: "I am so happy: I have the Lord Jesus in my heart!" This innocent testimony had its effect on the class, and boy after boy slipped outside. The master, standing on something to look out of the window, observed the boys kneeling in prayer around the schoolyard, each one apart. The master was overcome, so he asked the converted schoolboy to comfort them. Soon the whole school was in strange disorder, and the clergymen were sent for and remained all day dealing with seekers after peace, schoolboys, schoolgirls, teachers and parents and neighbours, the premises being thus occupied until eleven o'clock that night.

On June 7, 1859, an open-air meeting was held on Fair Hill to hear one or two of the converts. So many thousands attended that it was deemed advisable to divide the crowd into separate meetings, each addressed by an evangelical minister of one denomination or another. The people stood motionless until the very last moment, when an auditor cried in distress. Several others likewise became prostrated, bewildering the ministers, who, having had no similar experience previously, scarce knew how to help the distressed in soul and body. The clergymen spent all night in spiritual ministrations, and, when the sun arose, the following day was spent in like manner. A union meeting was launched and attracted the crowds for many months.

Dr. H. Grattan Guinness addressed more than 6,000 people in a single meeting in Coleraine. In August the work progressed steadily, and in September the churches were as full as ever. By October there were very few cases of prostration, but the prayer-meetings continued as numerous and well attended as before. Said the *Coleraine Chronicle* in a leader, "No one can deny that a change for the better, which all must believe to be permanent, has taken place in the case of hosts of individuals..." In 1860 the Grand Jury of the Coleraine Quarter Sessions was informed by the presiding judge that, in His Worship's opinion, only the moral and religious movement of the previous summer accounted for the reduction of crime to almost negligible proportions, there having been only one case (of an unimportant character) to try.

The Revival spread into the towns and villages of County Derry, and reached the historic city of Londonderry, where it appeared with great suddenness among all denominations. It began on June 12 with the visit of Ballymena converts, who moved many hearers to tears. Further open-air meetings attracted up to 5,000 people. In County Tyrone the Revival spread rapidly southwards. The people of County Armagh experienced the movement in their towns and villages simultaneously with Tyrone, but later than in Antrim and Down and the city of Belfast.

In the ecclesiastical capital of Ireland, the city of Armagh, there was the usual evidence of strange happenings. On Wednesday, September 21, 1859, a prayer-meeting for all Ireland was arranged. People came from miles around, riding on the roofs of railway carriages and stowing away in cattle-trucks and goods-vans. Scenes at Armagh were overpowering, for 20,000 people assembled in a large field, to be addressed (in part) by a distinguished Englishman, the Hon. and Rev. Baptist Noel. In October the local ministers reported that "a great and good work of conviction and conversion" was progressing.

County Fermanagh shared in the Revival, though rather belatedly. Unlike the other northern counties, Fermanagh possessed 38 per cent Episcopalians and only 6 per cent other Protestants, chiefly Methodists, whilst there were 56 per cent Roman Catholics.

Outside the six northern counties the Revival movement was felt, but in a degree inversely proportionate to the Roman Catholic majority in each county as well as directly proportionate to the presence of Presbyterians, Methodists, Baptists, Congregationalists and Quakers among the Protestants. This was specially true of the remaining three of the nine counties of Ulster, Donegal, Monaghan and Cavan.

There was more encouragement around Dublin, which possessed a large Protestant population amounting to 22 per cent in the city itself, no less than 40 per cent in the suburbs around; and 20 per cent in the County of Dublin. When tidings of the Revival in Ulster reached the Irish capital many clergymen and ministers repaired thither. Among them was the Rev. J. Denham Smith of Kingstown (now named Dun Laoghaire, pronounced *Dun Leary*), who was profoundly moved by what he saw.

In September 1859 Christians in Kingstown had a new spirit of prayer which became the forerunner of blessing, and in October and November there were inquiries after salvation in every meeting. The union prayer-meeting in Dublin was supported by members of all three major evangelical denominations. The large Metropolitan Hall, seating about 3,000, was made the venue of special meetings, Spurgeon preaching there five times in January 1860, and the Rev. Samuel J. Moore of Ballymena giving his discourse on the Revival in the North. In April the Metropolitan Hall was opened on Tuesdays for free prayer, 3,000 attending and more than 100 inquirers convicted in each of the first three meetings. In July an "increasing interest" was reported from the Metropolitan Hall, inquirers undiminished in numbers, and Sunday open-air meetings attracted 3,000. Without a doubt the Protestant community was experiencing Revival.

On the whole the Revival movement in the south and west of Ireland had none of the startling effects of the Ulster Awakening; nevertheless the work of grace among the isolated Protestant communities launched out many eager and faithful evangelists, clerical and lay, who laboured against overwhelming odds for the evangelization of their Roman Catholic fellow-countrymen.

The Hon. and Rev. Baptist Noel told a conference of the Evangelical Alliance that he thought that 100,000 converts in the Ulster Revival was probably under the mark. In all Ireland, there were more. Thus it was that the movement, which originated in a prayer-meeting of four young men in the village schoolhouse of Kells in the parish of Connor in the county of Antrim, made a greater impact spiritually on Ireland than anything reported since the days of Saint Patrick. Its effects are felt among the Protestants of Ireland until this day.

CHAPTER SIX

THE AWAKENING IN SCOTLAND

THE General Assembly of the Church of Scotland, held in Edinburgh in May 1860 after a year's observation of the Awakening, unanimously approved an Overture on Revivals of religion:

"The General Assembly, taking into consideration the gratifying evidences manifested in many countries, and in various districts of our own land, of an increased anxiety about salvation and deepening interest in religious ordinances, followed in so many cases by fruits of holy living, desires to record its gratitude to Almighty God..."

In the same month of May the General Assembly of the equally large Free Church of Scotland met in the same capital city and heard a moving address by the incoming Moderator, Dr. James Buchanan of Glasgow:

"Two years ago, our Assembly was deeply stirred by the intelligence of what God was doing in the United States of America. One year ago, the impression was deepened... the pregnant cloud had swept onwards and was sending down upon Ireland a plenteous rain. This year, the same precious showers have been and are even now falling within the limits of our own beloved land.

"We, as a Church, accept the Revival as a great and blessed fact. Numerous and explicit testimonies from ministers and members alike bespeak the gracious influence on the people. Whole congregations have been seen bending before it like a mighty rushing wind."

And in the same month of May the Synod of the United Presbyterian Church, the third largest church organization in Scotland:

"... resolved to recognize the hand of God in the measure of new life outpoured upon our churches, and appointed the second Sabbath of July as a special Day of Prayer for the Revival."

Thus the three main branches of the dominant Presbyterianism of Scotland, whose adherents formed 70 per cent of the total population, declared in no uncertain way that Scotland was experiencing a Revival of religion as striking as the movement in neighbouring Ulster; and at that time there were three times as many Protestants as in Ulster, for Scotland's population approximated 3,000,000.

As in Ireland, many were the preparations for Revival. Already the Christian life of Scotland was being quickened by evangelists, often drawn from the higher ranks of society. The news of the Revival of religion in the United States provoked much interest and not a few united prayer-meetings, as in Edinburgh, Glasgow, and Aberdeen, where there was united intercession for an abundant outpouring of the Holy Spirit. An example of the measure of prayer in preparation of heart for Revival is found in the official report of the United Presbyterian Church that one in every four of its 162,305 communicants was attending its regular prayer-meetings, an average of 40,549 members at prayer in 1,205 regular meetings; and 129 new prayer-meetings and an increase of 16,362 regular attenders developed in 1859.

News of the religious awakening in Ulster quickened the interest of Scottish Christians already stirred by the reports from America, and the main development of the movement seemed to come from America via Ulster to Scotland. An observer (the Rev. Adam Byth of Girvan) was later struck by the fact that the union prayer-meeting in New York (itself a product of the American Awakening) was requested to pray for the spiritual needs of Coleraine in Ulster. The union prayer-meeting in Coleraine (a product of the resultant Revival in Ulster) in turn was asked to pray for the spiritual welfare of Port Glasgow on the Clyde, which soon afterwards was in the throes of a Revival movement. Such were the spiritual links in an interesting chain.

Spiritual sympathy expressed in prayer knows no barriers of race or space. But that does not mean that racial affinity and geographical proximity played no part in the spread of the mid-nineteenth- century Awakening. The Scotch-Irish of America (Ulster emigrants) had played a leading part in the colonization of America and the establishment of the United States: it was to be expected that their kith and kin across the Atlantic in Ulster should have become the first community in Britain to be moved by the same sort of religious fervour. Likewise the majority of Ulster-Scots who had built the prosperous communities of Northern Ireland were immigrants from south-western Scotland, chiefly from the shores of the Firth of Clyde: it was to be expected that the same Revival would spread via their cousins across the North Channel from Galloway to Glasgow. Such was the case, for south-western Scotland in general, and its hub, Glasgow, in particular, were soon quickened extraordinarily in matters religious.

By the middle of August 1859 the Revival became news in Glasgow with all the suddenness of a summer thunderstorm. Three-quarters of a column was devoted to a report of a public meeting held in the City Hall, which crowded gathering was presided over by Bailie Playfair. Then the secular press reported a similar meeting—to hear about the Revival—in the Stockwell Free Church in the city, a meeting crowded to excess in which the interest was so deepened that tears and great excitement were in evidence. Four days later, at 6:30 p.m. on August 19, a public meeting was held on Glasgow Green, and the *North British Daily Mail* reported that approximately 20,000 people were present, crushing and pushing to hear the speakers.

Religious writers were very little ahead of secular in recognizing the sudden outbreak of Revival in Glasgow. The *Scottish Guardian* of August 2, 1859 claimed that

"The Holy Spirit has been manifesting His gracious power in a remarkable manner in this neighbourhood during *the last five days*. Our readers are aware that ever since the news of the Great Revival in America reached Scotland, prayer-meetings for the special purpose of imploring a similar blessing have been held in Glasgow as well as in other places. The intelligence which has reached us recently leaves no room to doubt that these prayers have been heard."

The report referred to increased attendances at prayer-meetings as well as increased numbers of conversions among those waiting behind for the counsel of the ministers and workers present. Three weeks later the same weekly paper commented on the increased attendance at union prayer-meetings. As in America and in Ireland, the union prayer-meetings at noon had their outcome in prayer-meetings and preaching services in the various evangelical churches on week-nights, and in these meetings there were scores of reported conversions.

After a year of the movement, Glasgow was still enjoying "times of refreshing", as a typical report will illustrate:

"Every Sabbath evening since the Bridgate Church was opened, the crowds around the stone pulpit have been increasing, until on Sabbath evening last, there could not have been fewer than 7,000 hearers, and probably more. We say 'hearers', for, notwithstanding the vastness of the congregation, the voice of the preacher appeared to be perfectly audible at the furthest extremity.

"At the close of the open-air service, an invitation is given from the pulpit to all who wish to come to a decision in the matter of religion to attend the prayer-meeting... Within ten minutes the church is generally packed, and, being seated for 900, it will receive probably upwards of 1,100 when thus crowded.

"About ten o'clock, the meeting was brought to a close, and those only were asked to remain who wished conversation with the minister and other friends. About 500 waited including, of course, the friends of those who were in distress. This meeting continued till a quarter from twelve o'clock."

Just as "approximately 20,000" had gathered on Glasgow Green at the beginning of the movement, a similar-sized crowd gathered on September 6, 1860. An adjoining theatre was opened for enquirers. The outstanding speaker, whose powerful voice seemed to fill the Green, was a butcher named Robert Cunningham.

So great was the interest and so heavy the work entailed thereby that three of the visiting speakers of note, Gordon Forlong, Reginald Radcliffe and Richard Weaver, collapsed with fatigue.

The Awakening of 1959-60 permeated every corner of southwestern Scotland down to the vale of Dumfries and the borders o Cumberland. The movement repeated all the phenomena of the Ulster movement, but most reports noted seemed to stress the dispensability of "prostrations" and other physical phenomena, recognizing their value in first startling the observers, but relieved when they gave way to quieter manifestations of conviction.

In the New Year of 1861 a second wave of revival blessing was felt in the Vale of Dumfries and in Glasgow. The occasion was the visit of a young American student of theology, Edward Payson Hammond, who was invited to conduct Revival services in Annan on the Solway Firth. The *Dumfries Standard* stated that the Revival spirit had reached a degree of intensity unparalleled in the religious history of the burgh. Young Hammond, his assistant Drysdale, four ministers, and many helpers often had to help inquirers (as many as 500 at a time) until the early hours of the morning. The work among children was noteworthy, and this factor shaped Mr. Hammond as a children's evangelist in future years. In Dumfries a secular paper described the movement as "marvellous". Payson Hammond carried the Revival influence again to Glasgow, where such a work was wrought that a thanksgiving meeting in the City Hall attracted 4,000 people and turned away twice as many more. The effect of Hammond's preaching was felt for many months in the communities visited, and permanent results of a gratifying order were claimed by his sponsors. The chief result of his ministry was the creation of an interest in Child Conversion.

The Highland Revival, sweeping up the western islands and the northern highlands, jumped across the Pentland Firth to the Orkney Islands, from which a Kirkwall gentleman reported: "There is a most marvellous, miraculous work of God's Spirit going on here... I believe that the whole character of this end of the island is changed." In 1860 there were eight special prayer-meetings in the Shetlands, and the general interest grew until 1862, when Dr. Craig and Mr. John Fraser began an evangelistic campaign to which up to 1,200 people came, overcrowding the parish church night after night. This work continued for many months into the spring of 1863, spreading from the town to the rural districts.

In north-east Scotland, from the Moray Firth to the Firth of Tay, including the counties of Nairn, Moray, Banff, Aberdeen, Kincardine and Angus, the Awakening was felt immediately and intensely in 1859. Following the prayer-movement in 1858, and the limited Revival in early 1859, there were ambitious open-air services in the city of Aberdeen in the spring and summer of 1859. London religious editors were credibly informed that there was scarcely a town or village between Inverness and Aberdeen that had not been visited by the quickening power of the Spirit. As to the nature of these awakenings, the Rev. W. T. Ker of Deskford stated:

"It is indeed a most wondrous work of the Lord, and it is passing along this whole coast like a mighty wave, having assumed a character identical with that of the work in Ireland."

Almost every parish in the county of Perth felt the

quickening influences of the Spirit during the wonderful years of 1859-60. Wherever there was a living Christian community the Revival was long prayed-for and its arrival hailed with gratification. More than fifty pastors and lay workers addressed about 4,000 people between 11 a.m. and 6 p.m. on one occasion (August 22, 1860), in which the sponsors declared that they "buried sectarianism in the South Inch of Perth that day, and saw no Christian weep over its grave". Church of Scotland, Church of England, United Presbyterian, Baptist and Independent pastors participated. In the City Hall 2,000 attended and simultaneously three other churches were used that evening, and many inquirers were dealt with by the pastors. Seven weeks later local ministers reported no abatement of the movement, "all the country round on fire".

There was a remarkable outbreak of Revival phenomena in Fifeshire, to the south of Dundee. An Army officer of high rank summed up his impressions of what he had seen in Cellardyke thus:

"Those of you who are at ease have little conception of how terrifying a sight it is when the Holy Spirit is pleased to open a man's eyes to see the real state of his heart.

"Men who were thought to be, and who thought themselves to be good, religious people... have been led to search into the foundation upon which they were resting, and have found all rotten, that they were self-satisfied, resting on their own goodness, and not upon Christ. Many turned from open sin to lives of holiness, some weeping for joy for sins forgiven."

The forerunner of the Edinburgh Revival was a united

prayer-meeting commenced in April 1858—when the news of the American Revival crossed the Atlantic—held every Monday for twenty-one months, becoming a daily prayer-meeting in January 1860. In this meeting, Church of Scotland, Free Church and United Presbyterian ministers worked together in happy unity.

In November it was reported from Edinburgh that "a very general expectation of a manifest outpouring of the Holy Spirit exists". Professor Charles G. Finney, American revivalist, was in Edinburgh for a short visit at that date and his meetings were exceedingly well attended, producing many converts. Strange things were already happening in the Carrubber's Close Mission (which had opened its doors eighteen months before by ejecting an Atheist Club from the premises) where scores of people of all ages were being converted. Only two of these displayed physical manifestations. Before long the influence of the work began to radiate in all directions, churches opening their doors to the "converts".

By March 1860 the work of Revival was making progress in Edinburgh and the surrounding district, prayer-meetings having been established in many towns and villages nearby, as well as in the city. Evangelistic meetings began to attract huge crowds, with happy results. Radcliffe and Weaver, English evangelists, could not get a place large enough for their meetings. On one occasion, 1,800 people crowded the Richmond Place Chapel, whilst thousands more packed the street outside. Weaver and Radcliffe had to walk on the shoulders of stalwart men in order to alternate in ministry inside and outside the chapel. Hundreds remained behind for conversation, even though the preaching had gone on intermittently from seven until eleven p.m.

In the Border Counties south of Edinburgh the Awakening began with prayer-meetings, which were quickened by news brought by their ministers from Northern Ireland and western Scotland.

In 1860 the remark was made that "this Revival is everywhere assuming the form of a great Home Mission". What had begun as an increase of prayer and intercession among the Christians became a great movement for the evangelization of Scotland. The incoming Moderator of the Free Church of Scotland in 1861 (Dr. Candlish) paid tribute to the quality of the work:

"Fathers and Brethren, I congratulate you on your meeting again in the midst of an outpouring of the Spirit of God, and a remarkable work of grace pervading the whole church and the whole land."

Judging from available material, there was not the same degree of controversy in Scotland as in Ireland about the work. This might be due to the fact that the manifestations in Ireland were completely novel in the experience of all. Scottish leaders knew what to expect.

Five years after the initial outbreak of the Revival a typical Presbytery Report noted the following points (summary ours):

(1) The Awakening had continued throughout the years, and was not so much a completed period of Revival but rather the beginning of a better state of things in the spread of vital religion.

(2) All classes came under its influence, and only at its earliest stages was it accompanied by much excitement.

(3) The agency was both lay and clerical, and the method both united prayer and expository preaching.

(4) The Revival had resulted in the quickening of believers, the increase of family religion, the decrease of cases of discipline in all the congregations since 1859.

The report added that whilst special conversions of a remarkable character had stood the test of time, it was difficult to state accurately what proportion of the total number of converts had been genuine as no attempt had been made in the first place to count such conversions. It is difficult to compile accurate statistics of real conversions in the Scottish Revival of 1859-60—not only because of the division and varying standards in Presbyterianism, but because the masses of ordinary people in customary formal membership in the Kirk provided most of the converts and were seldom noted as accessions.

A well-known evangelist was quoted as saying that thousands stood of the fruit of 1859-60, and many were going on well; and another added that in the first stages of the revival there was a seeking to the evangelist, whereas later it became a seeking of the lost by the evangelist.

The Presbyterian church in Ireland had incompletely reported an accession of 10,000 members in the first three months of the Ulster Revival, distributed among 300 of its 500 congregations. The United Presbyterian church in Scotland reported that 477 of their congregations added 15,314 new members presumably in the latter months of 1859. Both churches showed that 10 per cent was added to their total strength, this percentage may be considered typical of the Presbyterian bodies. It is remarkable that the average gain per congregation in the period of Revival was approximately the same in both cases—33.

The Revival, now *The Christian*, was the real day-to-day historian of the movement, and its trusted correspondents summer up in 1865:

"The wave of Divine blessing came to us apparently from Ireland four or five years ago. It struck first the west coast of Scotland, then spread over a great part of the country. It was a very blessed season, perhaps the most extensive in its operation that we have ever known amongst us. But it has, in a great measure, passed away. Still the fruits remain-living, active, consistent Christians who keep together, cherishing the memory of the time, blessing and praying for its return... The number of students entering our divinity halls this season will be double or triple that of former years; this is a blessed fruit of the Revival. Such men are likely to be of the right stamp..."

It was to a revived and prepared Scottish Church that the greatest product of the Revival, in its American phase, came—Dwight L. Moody, who found a well-ploughed field in which to sow the seed and reap a harvest fifteen years later.

CHAPTER SEVEN

THE AWAKENING IN WALES

THE 1859 Revival in Wales can be traced to the influence of the American Revival of 1858, but, unlike its Scottish counterpart, it owed nothing to the influence of the Ulster movement. Indeed, there is evidence to suggest that the outbreak of Revival phenomena in Wales actually preceded those experienced in Ulster. Nevertheless pride of place must be given to the Ulster movement on account of its influence upon the remainder of the United Kingdom, for English and Scottish religious life was comparatively uninfluenced by happenings in Cymric-speaking Welsh churches. In fact, in the summer of 1859, thousands of English Christians travelled through North Wales to embark at Holyhead on their way to study the work of grace in Ireland, without realizing that as profound an Awakening was stirring the villages and towns passed by whose inhabitants spoke the incomprehensible Welsh.

The literature of the 1859 Revival in Wales is meagre, even in the vernacular. Most of the Welsh accounts of the 1859 Revival partake more of the nature of poetic raptures than of sober-stated facts. It would be well to begin instead with a statement by a border-county Englishman, the Rev. John Venn, M.A., Prebendary of Hereford, read before the Evangelical Alliance gathering in the autumn of 1860. In it he claimed that almost every county in the principality had been influenced by a more or less remarkable work of grace. He endeavoured to assess the lasting worth of the movement by giving in detail the great numbers already received into full church membership by the various orthodox denominations. On the basis of figures given by various authorities, and adding a proportionate number for additions in the Established Church (his own denomination), Prebendary Venn estimated that about 100,000 persons in all had been received into full communion in the course of two years. Carefully, he was willing to deduct 10 per cent or so to avoid going beyond the truth, a deduction which could be ignored if one desired to estimate the numbers of professed conversions rather than additions to church membership, for it can be clearly demonstrated that great numbers of actual church members are professedly converted in every Revival movement.

In his *History of Protestant Nonconformity in Wales*, published in 1861, Thomas Rees states the number of conversions in the Revival of Nonconformists alone as being between 85,000 and 95,000, adding that "the numerous converts with comparatively rare exceptions holds on remarkably well". Fifty years after the Revival a reliable authority declared upon the basis of additions to church membership that it could be "safely accepted that the whole harvest of the Revival in Wales did not fall short of a hundred thousand souls", the great majority of whom satisfied the test of time. Thus approximately one-tenth of the population of Wales was permanently influenced by the Revival, for there were about 1,000,000 people in Wales in 1859.

"Before the '59 Revival," said Principal T. C. Edwards, D.D., of Bala, "the churches were withering away in our country; a wave of spiritual apathy and practical infidelity had spread over Wales." In the year following the Revival the number of criminal cases before the Welsh Courts decreased from 1,809 to 1,228.

How did such a movement so fraught with good originate? A Welsh lad named Humphrey Rowland Jones was born in North Cardiganshire about the year 1832. Fifteen years later he became converted, and in 1854 he applied to the Wesleyan District Meeting (South Wales) for admission to the ministry. He was rejected, and emigrated to the United States to join his parents. The Methodist Episcopal Church ordained him there.

Caught up in the American Revival movement in 1858, Humphrey Jones became a revivalist preacher, and as such returned to Wales in the summer of 1858. His evangelistic labours had a measure of success, but his success created unconcerned and good-natured scepticism in the mind of a neighbouring Calvinistic Methodist minister, David Morgan, who distrusted anything of American extraction and Wesleyan communication.

The Rev. David Morgan himself had been awakened in a local Revival in his native Cardiganshire in 1841. His ministry was recognized in 1857, when he was ordained by the Trevine Association. For ten years he had prayed for an outpouring of the Divine Spirit. Hence, in spite of his prejudice, he went to hear young Humphrey Jones at a Wesleyan Chapel nearby Ysbytty Ystwyth and was deeply convicted by an address on the words: "Because thou art neither hot nor cold, I will spue thee out of my mouth." David Morgan entered into an experience of spiritual deepening a few days later.

In David Morgan's village, Ysbytty Ystwyth, the population did not exceed 1,000, yet 200 adult converts had been won before the end of 1858. A feature of the Revival was *moliannu* or *praising*, a peculiar form of worship which might be described as a chorus of rapturous praise from preacher and people together. In early 1859 David Morgan began to visit neighbouring village churches. In Pontrhydfendigaid more than half the population of 800 united themselves to the Calvinistic Methodist church. An unordained Pontrhydfendigaid lad carried the "infection" to Tregaron, where the congregation burst into *praising* and eighty-seven people were converted in the service. By midsummer the whole county of Cardigan had become pervaded with the most fervid religious feeling, and the Calvinistic Methodist converts alone numbered 9,000 in June, 15,000 in August, in a population of 70,000.

Every county in Wales experienced blessing. Following the week of prayer in January 1860, a second wave of Revival swept Wales, with greater strength in some places, and with the same happy inter-denominational unity.

In Monmouthshire—culturally a Welsh county though part of England—the Revival movement may be traced to the Congregational Association meetings at Beaufort, June 29 and 30, 1859.

Cardiff, the Welsh metropolis, shared in the evangelistic movements stirring England in the 1860s. In 1862, in the spring, Dr. and Mrs. Walter C. Palmer (American evangelists) began to experience stirring times in Cardiff. For thirty days "a remarkable work of the Spirit" was acknowledged and felt throughout the town, affecting public morals and bringing hundreds to the house of prayer, so much so that a town councillor (Anglican) of long experience testified that police cases were dwindling and a detective added that Cardiff had become a different place. The local ministers supported the work well, and 800 people became inquirers in their churches. The Palmers were followed by Richard Weaver, and "half the people could not get in": the largest building in South Wales, the Music Hall, was filled with 4,000 people each evening, and hundreds were turned away.

In the spring of 1863 William and Catherine Booth, fresh from Revival meetings of great power in Cornwall, began preaching in Cardiff, and won 500 people to the faith. Mrs. Booth preached with simplicity and modesty. So great was the interest in the Booth campaign that it became necessary to use a large circus building accommodating between 2,000 and 3,000 people. The effort was supported by Christians of every denomination. Quite a number of the converts of the Cardiff meetings were Cornish people, one couple having travelled by sea to Wales on account of conviction produced by the Revivalist in Cornwall. The Booths were followed by Richard Weaver on another visit, and crowds of 3,000 attended nightly, 500 of whom professed decision.

It should be emphasized that in all these Cardiff campaigns English was the medium of preaching. The reports of Revival in Cardiff during the earlier Welsh Revival movement are so scarce that it underlines the notion that Cardiff was looked upon as a cosmopolitan city within Wales. That the English movements of the 1860s affected Cardiff so powerfully bears this out.

The Calvinistic Methodist Church of Wales (now the Presbyterian Church of Wales) reaped a rich harvest from the Revival of 1859. The number of converts who subsequently joined their churches were 36,190.

The Congregationalists claimed a similar total of converts gained by their churches, about 36,000. In the single county of Carnarvon the Congregationalists built a score of new chapels to house the increased attendance.

The Baptist churches gained about 14,000 new members from the converts. The Rev. Thomas Thomas, Principal of the Baptist College at Pontypool, reported "tens of thousands" of additions, and many new churches formed for Welsh-speaking and English-speaking adherents. Double the usual number of students for the Baptist ministry began studies in Pontypool and Haverfordwest.

The Wesleyan Methodists in Wales gained 4,549 new members in 1859-60. The Church of England in Wales supported the movement, but its gains were only estimated, no reliable figures being available. The estimate suggested 20,000 new communicants.

It can be demonstrated that the Welsh Revival of 1859 was almost wholly unrelated, historically and geographically, to the Irish and Scottish Revivals of the same period. It owed nothing to them. However, the Welsh Revival of 1859 displayed many features of spiritual kinship with the contemporary movements in Ireland and Scotland, and all three derived inspiration from the American movement of 1858.

The Rev. D. Charles of Trevecca College outlined three main characteristics of the Welsh Revival thus: firstly, an extraordinary spirit of prayer among the masses; secondly, a remarkable spirit of union among all denominations of Christians; and thirdly, a powerful missionary effort for the conversion of others. These three characteristics were displayed by the American, Irish and Scottish movements. Another remarkable affinity of movement is noticed in the fact that the Welsh Revival of 1859 was independent of great personalities. Even David Morgan the Revivalist, who was signally used in the inception and spread of the movement, was a simple country pastor.

In what ways did the Welsh movement differ from its contemporaries? There were fewer cases of physical prostration in Wales, but just as many evidences of intense conviction or agony of mind. In Ulster the physical prostrations were the stimulating incidents which created public interest; in Wales, the rapturous praise seemed to be the crisis point in each locality.

Take, for example, the outbreak of Revival in a Carmarthenshire town, as recorded by the son of David Morgan.

"One Sunday morning, an elder rose to speak, and his first remark was that the God they worshipped was without beginning and without end. 'Amen!' exclaimed a young girl in the highest notes of a lovely voice. 'Blessed be His name forever.'

"This cry might be compared to the touch of the electric button that shivers a quarry into a thousand hurtling fragments. Scores leaped from their seats, and, gathering in the vacant space in the centre, they gave vent to their pent-up emotions in outcries that were almost agonizing in their ardour and intensity."

Time and time again in the Morgan narrative one is struck with the recurrence of a purely oratorical stimulus which provoked a storm of praise, in which the already-converted half of the congregation indulged in unrestrained ejaculatory utterance and the unconverted half fell under the deepest conviction. The explanation must come from an analysis of the Cymric *psyche*, the vehicle of the spiritual impulse.

CHAPTER EIGHT

THE AWAKENING IN ENGLAND

THE PATTERN of the Awakening in England was noteworthy, for it included fullscale Revival of the spontaneous and immediate type experienced in Ulster, Wales and Scotland; other movements following the metropolitan London pattern; and delayed-action movements which took several years before the Revival produced the right atmosphere and leaders for general aggressive evangelism.

North of the Tyne in Northumberland, late in the summer of 1859, there was an early stirring due to the visit of Dr. and Mrs. Walter C. Palmer. The Palmers had been witnesses of the original outbreak of Revival in the city of Hamilton, Ontario, in 1857- the very first instance of unusual power of conviction in the movement which afterwards swept around the world. The visit of these American Methodists provided a fitting climax to twelve months of prayer-meetings, for intercession had been going on in Newcastle from the time of the arrival of news of the American Revival, a preparation which placed Tyneside in the same position as Ulster, Scotland and Wales rather than most parts of England.

The Times (of London) reported "A Religious 'Revival' at Newcastle-on- Tyne" in a headline, adding that

"... this town has become the scene of a religious 'Awakening' which bids fair to rival anything of the kind which has occurred either in America or the North of Ireland."

By October 1859 there seemed to be a more or less general awakening going on in the Tyneside city, Anglican and Nonconformist clergy and ministers conducting special services, in one of which (a Methodist church) an owner of saloons and investor in the brewery business created a sensation by renouncing all connection with the liquor traffic. During the same month the Rev. Robert Young reported:

"The Revival with which this town is favoured is advancing with increased power and glory. In Brunswick Place Chapel we hold a daily united prayer-meeting from twelve o'clock to one; another meeting for exhortation and prayer, from three to five; and a similar service from seven to ten. Many seemed 'filled with the Holy Ghost', and pray 'as the Spirit gives them utterance'. All attempts to proselytize are utterly repudiated: hence some designate the work 'the Evangelical Alliance Revival'. The meetings, though often crowding our spacious chapel, are orderly, and generally marked by deep solemnity. It is true that, occasionally, there is the cry of the spirit-stricken sinner, and the bursting joy of the newly-emancipated captive... but that is music in our ears."

Within a month this minister was reporting further that the Newcastle Awakening had accounted for 1,300 conversions in his church, all the converts being willing to publish their names. At the end of the year Mr. Young reported that there were 1,400 converts of the Brunswick Chapel special services alone, confirmed or checked.

Five years later in Newcastle the work of God was reported "going on gloriously among our working men". 1865 evangelism in Newcastle was still effective in church and public hall.

In the county of Durham, there was an immediate response to the prayer challenge of 1859-60. In Sunderland, during August 1859, a meeting of ministers resolved unanimously:

"1. Regarding with profound gratitude the wonderful displays of Divine power in the religious Awakenings of America, Ireland, Scotland, and Wales (this meeting) is of the opinion that special congregational prayer-meetings should be held *simultaneously* in our several places of worship, to direct attention to the spiritual signs of the blessing times in which we live, and to pray for a Revival of religion in our own town.

"2. That the week commencing Monday, September 5 be selected for these godly exercises, and that the several churches in our town be recommended to arrange for as many congregational prayer-meetings as possible, during the five days from September 5 to 9."

September 1859 prayer-meetings were held generally "morning, noon and night" in Sunderland, well-attended by professing Christians and anxious inquirers after salvation. The first phase of the Revival had begun. Later in the year the ministers claimed that an extensive visitation had moved Sunderland. No less than 3,444 persons joined the local Wesleyan Societies in a movement led by Dr. and Mrs. Palmer from the United States.

Another fruitful centre of Revival and evangelism in County Durham was the Tyneside city of Gateshead. The Palmers visited the city in May 1860, winning 500 or more converts. A New Connexion (Methodist) Church there experienced a time of Revival in 1859 under its pastor, William Booth. Four years later a circuit chapel reported that of the forty-nine professed conversions occurring within its walls that year thirty cases were known to have joined the society, of whom eleven were still in fellowship, another fourteen were in fellowship elsewhere, and another three had just been restored from backsliding, showing a loss of only two out of the thirty. In the second phase of the Revival, 1861, 200 conversions were reported, making the total in the three years 300 new members added to the New Connexion circuit. So many sinners were brought to repentance that the Bethesda Chapel earned the name of "The Converting Shop". It was during these Revival times that Mrs. Catherine Booth (January 8, 1860) announced her intention of preaching— to the astonishment of her husband and his congregation. Likewise it was during this Revival that William and Catherine Booth began to preach the doctrine of Full Salvation, now an integral part of Salvationist teaching. The Booths also conducted a preaching mission in Hartlepool, attracting up to 1,000 people, turning many away disappointed, and winning 250 converts. In spite of this success, the Methodist New Connexion Conference tried to set a limit on Booth's evangelism, leading to his resignation in 1862.

Dr. and Mrs. Palmer campaigned in Carlisle in February 1860, their work being soon reported as "The Revival in Carlisle". A year later there was a further movement, attributed to the melting and subduing influence of the Holy Spirit, in which numbers of converted youths were found bringing in "the young heathen" from the streets. Throughout January 1861 this movement bore fruit in the conversion of young people chiefly; six months later the work of grace was still on the increase, supported by a united meeting of five churches for purposes of prayer, and effected by the hiring of a local theatre for purposes of preaching.

In the 1860s evangelism was continuing in strength in Liverpool, with meetings of between 700 and 1,000 young men, producing results in conversions. E. Payson Hammond, the American evangelist, visited Liverpool in the summer of 1861 and addressed large gatherings, following which hundreds of inquirers remained for conversation. Another American, J. W. Bonham of Massachusetts, held successful meetings in Bootle and Liverpool. In the autumn Reginald Radcliffe began Sunday evening meetings in the Concert Hall, which was overflowing. About the same time the Americans, Dr. and Mrs. Palmer, came to Liverpool for a rest from their heavy labours, and were immediately caught up in "an extraordinary work of the Holy Spirit" not confined to any particular denomination, with converts numbered in the hundreds. On Christmas Eve, 1859, Professor Charles Grandison Finney, of Oberlin College in Ohio, arrived in Bolton with Mrs. Finney, and became a spearhead of the Revival movement there among Congregationalists and Methodists. The chapel was filled from the first meeting, and Professor Finney called for inquirers on the fourth night and found the vestry filled. The meetings were transferred to a large Temperance Hall, and under Finney's able direction the whole town was canvassed with happy results. Three months later more than 1,200 were attending the weeknight services and hundreds were being turned away on Sundays. A report noted:

"The Rev. C. G. Finney, by whom these services are conducted... is close upon seventy years of age. His style of address is singularly direct. There is a total absence of display, and a complete forgetfulness, on most occasions at least, of the graces of elocution. There is the most rigid exactness of statement, the severest simplicity, the closest reasoning, and the discourse proceeds step by step, the judgment of the hearer forced along with it, until the end."

The Bolton newspaper remarked upon the union of effort of Churchmen and Dissenters, and stated that some 2,000 conversions had been accomplished, 400 in a single week. Finney's *Autobiography* records extremely interesting cases of conviction, confession, restitution and conversion, and tells of the theologian's efforts to restrain the more noisy Methodist workers. Before the end of the Finney campaign, the minister in charge of the canvassers claimed that the movement had reached every family in Bolton.

Following the Week of Prayer in Manchester and throughout the country in January 1860, a Manchester businessman visited various towns in Lancashire, including Bolton, and witnessed the unforgettable religious Revival under Charles G. Finney's ministry with maximum co-operation from the local pastors and members. In April the Finneys proceeded to Manchester, tired after their labours in Bolton, but hopeful of seeing a Revival movement break out in Manchester. Finney was disappointed, for he found a lack of unity of purpose between the Methodists and Congregationalists, and among the Congregationalists themselves. Nevertheless, large numbers of people professed conversion and the work increased in strength until August, when Finney left for America. A local observer confirmed Finney's own report of several hundreds professedly converted, stating that more than 100 inquirers remained after each service, though these must have included backsliders seeking restoration and professors of religion seeking Revival.

In Manchester the religious Revival appeared in full strength two years after the initial prayer-meetings. The work continued till the end of 1861, and there were strong testimonies to support the claim that the work was neither superficial nor evanescent.

One of the converts of the 1861 meetings was Henry Moorhouse, whose companions were as irreligious as himself. Moorhouse heard shouting and noise from within the Alhambra, buttoned up his coat ready for whatever fray was provided, and rushed in, only to be confronted by the sight of ex-pugilist Richard Weaver preaching the Gospel in his inimitable style. Before long Moorhouse and his companions had found the same "salvation" preached by Weaver, and Henry Moorhouse was launched on his career as a remarkable evangelist of world-wide reputation. In 1867 Harry Moorhouse crossed the Atlantic and began to preach in America. The story of his engagement with Dwight L. Moody is well known. For seven nights in succession Moorhouse preached the Gospel from John iii. 16: "For God so loved the world, that he gave his only begotten son, that whosoever believeth in him should not perish, but have everlasting life." Moody had preached more on the judgments of God than on His love, but the Ministry of Moorhouse changed him. Moorhouse taught Moody to draw his sword full length and Moody testified: "I have preached a different Gospel since."

Early in 1860 a London lady named Mrs. Elizabeth Codner published anonymously in *The Revival* a poem whose sentiments were so wistfully expressed that it became a well-known and much-used hymn wherever the English tongue is spoken. Its words provide us with a gauge of the feelings of London evangelicals about the Revival movements already under way in Ulster and Scotland and Wales:

> "Lord, I hear of showers of blessing
> Thou art scattering full and free;
> Showers the thirsty land refreshing:
> Let some droppings fall on me,
> Even me."

Dr. Eugene Stock, secretary of the Church Missionary Society and equally famed as a Deeper Life speaker in after years, declared in retrospect that the period under review was marked by a religious Revival of a kind unlike anything experienced in Britain since (with the exception of the localized Welsh Revival of 1905), adding that the most striking feature of the Revival of the 1860s was the phenomena of the prayer-meetings.

"I can never forget January 9, 1860, when, at nine o'clock on a bitterly cold morning, that hall was densely packed for nothing but simple prayer for the outpouring of the Holy Spirit."

The second week of January 1860 was devoted by multitudes of believers to special united prayer for an outpouring of the Holy Spirit all over the world. This feature of the Revival originated in an invitation issued in 1858 by a group of American missionaries in Ludhiana, a small town in North-West India, asking all Christians throughout the world to set aside the second week of 1860 for united prayer. The response of leaders and people to this call to prayer was as astonishing as it was spontaneous, for in London alone there were at least 200 united prayer- meetings.

The effect of united prayer upon Christians of all denominations is always the same. Towards God their hearts are stirred with love which finds expression in a Christian unity transcending the artificial boundaries of race, people, class, and creed; towards the outsiders their hearts are filled with love which sets out immediately, like the Good Shepherd, to bring the Lost Sheep into the fold.

The records of the movement in London are full of examples of the effect of prayer upon worship, fellowship, and evangelism, all of which revived immeasurably. The awakened Christians in London soon found an opportunity of harnessing the flowing tides of Revival to generate sufficient power to carry the Light to the most darkened masses of the metropolis. The prime mover in the matter was that "evangelical of the evangelicals", the Seventh Earl of Shaftesbury, who helped begin a series of theatre meetings, which he himself made possible by sponsoring the Religious Worship Act removing all legal impediments.

On New Year's Day, 1860, the Britannia, the Garrick, and Sadler's Wells Theatres were thrown open for Sunday evening services for the people, attracting "overwhelming" and "immense" audiences to hear sermons by both Established clergymen and Dissenting ministers. Another two theatres were opened later that month, and a couple more in February, by which time all seven were catering for an aggregate attendance nightly of more than 20,000. Special services for upper- and middle-class people were held in St. Paul's Cathedral and Westminster Abbey, and also in St. James's and Exeter Halls in the West End.

No numerical report is available concerning the aggregate of the vast but orderly crowds attending St.

Paul's Cathedral for special services, led by the Bishop of London, "with his usual zeal"; neither are any estimates given of the total attendance at the very similar services in Westminster Abbey. On the basis of sitting space and the report of crowded gatherings, an estimate of 100,000 during the season would be modest.

The seasonal aggregate attendance at the theatre services of the Shaftesbury United Committee appeared to be in excess of 250,000. Likewise, the Free Church theatre services held by Baptist, Congregationalist, Methodist and Presbyterian ministers in St. James's Hall, Piccadilly, and the Britannia Theatre in the East End, attracted an aggregate of 250,000 each winter.

Independently, services were begun in the Victoria Theatre, Waterloo, by Richard Weaver, and continued by William Carter. No less than 559 services were held in the first four winter seasons, with an aggregate of 865,100 people in attendance, an average seasonal aggregate of more than 200,00 in a single theatre! Sunday afternoon meetings for inquirers and converts were arranged, and an observer reported more than 400 present, whilst the evening meeting was "crammed to the roof". It is claimed that John Pearce, Esquire, founder of London's chain of "J.P." Restaurants, was converted in one of William Carter's mass meetings for the "unwashed". In April 1862 the converts' meetings filled the theatre and hundreds were turned away, and there were insufficient workers to deal with the many penitents in the evening.

Yet another committee known as the Additional Theatre Services Committee commenced work in four theatres-the Marylebone, Soho, Surrey and City of London theatres. It was usual for hundreds to remain for prayer, inquiry or decision-among them W. T. P. Wolston, afterwards the reputable Edinburgh physician. No figures seem available, but it is not unreasonable to credit these theatres with an aggregate attendance equal to the single effort at the Victoria Theatre, 200,000 seasonally.

Services in the Garrick Theatre in Whitechapel were taken over by the East London Special Services Committee, which arose from a conference called together on January 23, 1861, by Reginald Radcliffe in the Sussex Hall in Leadenhall Street to discuss the need of the East End of London. To some 200 Christians Baptist Noel truly prophesied:

"If this work is done, we shall see some unknown Luthers and Whitefields excavated out of this dark mine, to spread the Gospel farther and wider than we have any idea... I believe we are on the eve of a greater work than England ever saw, and the East End of London is the right place to begin."

Out of this East End of London venture grew the Salvation Army, a subject reserved for later treatment. No record of numbers reached by the East London Committee is available, either at the Garrick or the City of London Theatre, or elsewhere.

In addition to these organized committee-controlled activities were "numberless free special services in and around London". On the basis of the known figures alone, it can be safely said that some 50,000 of London's unchurched people were reached each Sunday in the theatre services, or *a million aggregate each season during the Revival.*

Nowhere in the stirring accounts of Revival in London was there any evidence of prostration or hysteria. The work in London seemed to have developed in a different form from that which preceded it in Ulster, Wales and Scotland. The London Revival of the early 1860s was one of preaching. The evangelistic campaigns which were held throughout the metropolis in the Revival years of the 1860s are too numerous to be chronicled here. Their results were manifold. In the Revival decade (prior to 1865) the Protestant churches of London added 200,000 sittings to their total accommodation, a 60 per cent increase which outstripped the fast-growing population of the metropolis by a small margin. In denominational reactions the impact of the 1859 Awakening upon the life of London was felt in many ways and through many channels.

Bishop Handley Moule, who became a close associate of Evan Hopkins in later years, recalled his impressions of the Dorset revival in which both were converted:

"I must not close without a memory, however meagre, of one wonderful epoch in the parish. It was the Revival. The year was 1859, that 'year of the right hand of the Most High'... Ulster was profoundly and lastingly moved and blessed. Here and there in England it was the same: and Fordington was one of the scenes of Divine Awakening.

"For surely it was Divine. No artificial means of excitement were dreamt of; my Father's whole genius was against it. No powerful personality, no Moody or Aitken, came to us. A city missionary and a London Bible-woman were the only helpers from a distance. But a power not of man brought souls to ask the old question: 'What must I do to be saved?' Up and down the village, the pastor, the pastoress, and their faithful helpers, as they went their daily rounds, found 'the anxious'. And the church was thronged to overflowing, and so was the spacious schoolroom, night after night throughout the week. The very simplest means carried with them a heavenly power. The plain reading of a chapter often conveyed the call of God to men and women, and they 'came to Jesus as they were'.

"I do not think I exaggerate when I say that hundreds of people at that time were awakened, awed, made conscious of eternal realities. And a goodly number of these showed in all their after life that they were indeed new creatures, born again to a living hope and to a stedfast walk. And 'the leaves of the tree were for healing' apart from the holy fruit of spiritual conversions. A great social uplifting, wholesome and permanent, followed the Revival."

The Revival was described by Handley Moule's biographers as a "mighty influence upon the mind of the growing boy, of which he would speak with enthusiasm to the end of his life". Shortly after the Revival the youngster proceeded to Cambridge with the impression of God indelibly marked upon his soul, and a few years later he declared himself openly.

Although instances of spontaneous Revival could be given in reports from all parts of Cornwall, the most effective work developed through the visit of William and Catherine Booth from outside the county. The Revival movement began at Hayle in the middle of August. No actual conversions were noted on the first Sunday, so the evangelist used his opportunity on Monday to speak to the believers on "Hindrances to Christian Joy". Nearly all the congregation that evening stayed for a prayer-meeting, and, after a second message, a woman made her way to "the anxious seat", becoming—in the hopes of the evangelist—"the first-fruits of what I trust will be a glorious harvest". Eighteen months later the convert in question had been followed by 7,000 others who professed decision under the challenge of this evangelist and his ministering wife, William and Catherine Booth.

A survey of the Booth missions in Cornwall in 1861 and 1862 was given space in the *Wesleyan Times*, stressing the remarkable conversions of sinners, the awakening of slumbering churches, and the perseverance of the converts. It was said:

"All the friends in every place unite in the delightful testimony that the results of the movement abide more generally than those of any other similar work in their past experience."

Yet this period of great fruitfulness in the lives of William and Catherine Booth is described as a "Wilderness" experience by General Booth's biographer, Harold Begbie. It will be conceded that William Booth was yet to do a greater work, but it ought to be said that the period of these Cornish Revivals 1861-2) was one of profoundest importance in the life of the founder of the Salvation Army, and one which must have shaped his ministry.

How did the Methodist churches show their appreciation of the Booths? In June 1862 the Methodist New Connexion Conference at Dudley accepted his resignation, disapproving his Revivalism. In the same month the Primitive Methodist Conference at Sheffield aimed a blow at his calling in a resolution urging all its pastors "to avoid the employing of Revivalists so-called". And the Wesleyan Conference next month at Camborne— in spite of the knowledge that Booth had added 4,247 new members to Wesleyan churches in Cornwall—directed its superintendents not to sanction the use of their chapels for continuous services by outsiders. It seems impossible to reject the opinion widely held in Cornwall that opposition to William Booth was caused by ministerial jealousy of a free-lance. So the Booths departed from Cornwall with the jeers of the Wesleyan President about "the perambulations of the male and female" ringing in their ears.

There were two phases of the Evangelical Awakening of 1859 in the middle belt of English counties, the first being the movement to prayer begun in the summer of 1859 and developed beyond description after the second week of January 1860, whereas the second was the evangelistic phase, sometimes following directly after the prayer movement but more often breaking out in the autumn of 1861 or later.

The twin cultural capitals of England, the Universities of Oxford and Cambridge, were profoundly moved by the prayer-meeting movement. In the autumn of 1859 a Universities Prayer Union was begun, and an appeal was made for special prayer for Revival in Oxford and Cambridge.

At that time Oxford University was anything but an evangelical stronghold. Wadham College was regarded as the evangelical college, and to Wadham came young Hay Aitken in 1861, fresh from his tour of evangelism in the Revival areas of northern Scotland. Hay Aitken and his friend Freeman vowed to speak to every Wadham undergraduate about his spiritual welfare. It seems likely that the ambitious evangelist extended his operations to the whole University, for one reads that (shortly before 1865)

"a sort of evangelical Revival amongst undergraduates had taken place, especially at Wadham, where W. Hay M.

H. Aitken, afterwards the famous missioner, had been in residence."

There was much the same sort of prayer-meeting movement in Cambridge, and an observer in 1863 reported:

"On Sunday evening I was in a prayer-meeting at Cambridge, nothing but undergraduates crying to God for wholehearted consecration."

Into the Oxford prayer fellowships was thrust a young undergraduate, Francis James Chavasse, an aspiring Christian whose own testimony against himself seems rather harsh: "proud, wilful, disobedient, selfish, and black with sin, I need to be cleansed..."

Young Chavasse was confirmed in 1863, and grew in grace through his Oxford experience, attending evangelistic meetings at the one and prayer-meetings at the other. Without doubt, the "sort of evangelical Revival" in Oxford helped shape his spiritual experience which made his life as Bishop of Liverpool what it was.

Into the Cambridge prayer fellowships was thrust Handley Carr Glyn Moule, impressed in the 1860 Dorsetshire Revival and soon to declare himself wholeheartedly as a servant of Christ. These two saintly Bishops are but two examples of the products of the Evangelical Awakening of the mid-nineteenth century upon the Universities.

In the West Midlands the clergy of the great city of Birmingham convened a general prayer-meeting late in 1859. In early 1863 Dr. and Mrs. Palmer, with Methodist co-operation, began holding special services at noontime and in the evening, with 133 inquirers recorded in the first six days. The movement spread to all denominations and affected a number of neighbouring towns and villages. They were followed in September of that year by another pair who had been inspired by their joint ministry at Gateshead—none other than William and Catherine Booth, who had a most successful time in the Moseley Street Chapel, with about 150 professed conversions. The Booths were followed by their friend and patron, the Rev. James Caughey, who had deeply impressive meetings in Bath Street Chapel and the Alhambra Circus, seating 3,000. Thus it might be said that Birmingham was one of those English towns which was evangelized, rather than revived, by the Awakening.

In 1863 a religious Revival began in the Black Country, that intensely industrialized area to the north of Birmingham. Dr. and Mrs. Palmer, the American evangelists, laboured for a month in Walsall, using the midday prayer-meeting and the evening preaching-service technique. As a result, 300 people made profession of conversion, including people as old as eighty years. Some of the converts requested prayer on behalf of their personal friends, and had the joy of seeing them make decision also.

The Palmers' visit to Walsall (February 1863) was followed by that of the Booths, who laboured there until the summer. One of William Booth's open-air meetings attracted about 5,000 people, three-quarters of whom were men, and upon these working men were turned loose a team of convert-preachers, as Booth wrote:

"… just of the stamp to grapple with this class, chiefly of their own order, talking to them in their own language, regarding themselves as illustrations of the power of the Gospel…"

One had been a drunken, gambling, prize-fighting hooligan who had needed five or six policemen to take him to jail. Another had been a horse-racer, professional gambler and drunkard. Yet another was nicknamed "the Birmingham Rough", a wicked and abandoned character before his conversion. That evening the local chapel was crowded to hear Catherine Booth speak, and some forty decisions were recorded there. It is interesting to note that one of the converts of the Walsall Mission was a lad, Bramwell Booth, who (without parental urging) came under conviction and joined the penitents.

In the autumn of 1863 William Booth was still labouring in the Black Country, and a letter to a friend describes his experiences in Cradley Heath (three miles from Dudley) whose population exceeded 20,000. The chapel was full the first Sunday morning, and was too overcrowded for comfortable speaking or hearing at night. William Booth began by calling upon the leaders of the church to make a renewed consecration of themselves to God, and "a gracious melting and breaking up of heart followed, blessing a great number throughout the chapel". Conversions began to be declared in the days that followed. Booth's account averred:

"At the commencement of the prayer-meeting, a sturdy-looking man (who had been coming to the chapel every night but going away hardening his heart) jumped on to a form, and speaking out before all the people, said,

"'Do you know me?'

"The praying men answered, 'Yes'.

"'What am I then?' he said.

"They replied, 'A backslider'.

"'Well, then,' said he, 'I will be a backslider no longer; all of you come to Jesus with me,' and he fell in an agony of prayer for God to have mercy upon him; indeed the anguish and desire of his soul was too much for him, for he swooned away on the floor before us all. His wife was one of the first converted the previous week, and only that evening had sent up a request that God would save her husband, who was a poor miserable backslider. About thirty that night professed to obtain mercy..."

At Walsall, William Booth's converts were announced to take part in the proceedings as the "Hallelujah Band". It was through their ministry that William Booth adopted a lasting principle, that the masses would be most effectively reached by their own kind. Indeed, a recent article written by an interested minister, the Rev. Joseph Pearce, claimed that the Walsall Revival Campaign influenced William Booth much more than historians admit. William Booth was the guest of an ardent local-preacher, the drainage inspector of the New British Iron Company, Palmer by name. According to Mr. Pearce,

"... the Palmers had a spacious garden in which William Booth walked for hours in the deepest thought, with head on chest. This happened so frequently that one day Mr. Palmer had the temerity to say,

"'Excuse me, Mr. Booth, but I cannot help wondering what it is that engages your thoughts so frequently and protractedly as you pace the garden.'

"Mr. Booth, with face all ashine, replied:

"'My friend, I am thinking out a plan, which, when it is implemented, will mean blessing to the wide, wide world'."

CHAPTER NINE

THE DENOMINATIONAL INGATHERING

THERE were thirty million people inhabiting the United States of America in 1858.[1] More than five million of these were communicants of the evangelical Protestant churches, the aggressive Methodist and Baptist bodies claiming fully three million members.

Dr. Frank G. Beardsley, in his *History of American Revivals* (1904), states that the numerical fruits of the I 858 Revival are estimated between three hundred thousand and one million converts, and in this statement he is echoed by a more recent historian, Grover C. Loud. Beardsley says that it is impossible to estimate with any degree of accuracy the numerical results, but places his opinion upon record that five hundred thousand would "in all probability" be "approximately correct" as an estimate. The historian, Bishop Candler, on the other hand, avers that fully one million were converted in the Revival, four hundred thousand having been brought to Christ in a single year. Bishop Candler bases his statement only upon estimates and opinions apparently, and makes no systematic attempt to prove his contentions, but, in the mind of the present historian, his summary is substantially correct.

The number of converts received into church

[1] *The U.S. Census* 1910, vol. i., p. 127, gives the figure 23,191,876 for 1850 and 31,443,321 for 1860.

membership by eight leading denominations in 1858 is available. Additions mount up to nearly four hundred thousand in 1858, this without counting new members received by letter. Collection of these figures proved a wearisome though fascinating task. Besides these are incomplete returns from smaller bodies, raising by mathematical calculation the sum total for the year 1858 to half a million for all evangelical bodies. By similar methods, the total for the twenty-four months following the first outbreak of Revival late in 1857 is calculated at more than a million converts.

Considering the year 1858 alone, the records show that the total increase was apportioned in the following manner:

The greatest gainers were the Methodist churches. In the year 1858, the Methodist Episcopal Church received by profession of faith 135,517 new members, while the Methodist Episcopal Church South received 43,338 additions. Between them, these two Methodist bodies found that no less than twelve per cent of their members were converts of the Revival in that single year. Other Methodist church bodies gained proportionately, making a total of over 200,000 converts.

The second largest denominational group, the Baptists, gained 92,243 members by baptism in 1858, which is ten per cent of total membership. The Free Will Baptists gained 5,714 by baptism in 1858, again over ten per cent of membership for that year. The total number of believers baptized is incompletely given as 111,647 and a proportionate calculation for the smaller Baptist bodies would bring the total to 150,000 baptisms.

The Presbyterian figures for additions by examination (omitting those by letter) is given at 34,650; Congregational

Churches at 21,582; the Protestant Episcopal Church at 14,822; the Dutch Reformed and other Presbyterian bodies at 10,065. These additions by examination or profession are slightly less than ten per cent of recorded church membership.

The total of converts who joined the churches in 1858 is approximately ten per cent of the total church membership. Of five million evangelical Christians, five hundred thousand, therefore, were the fruits of the Revival in that single year. This contention is borne out by the fact that the above-mentioned denominations whose figures are available give a total of 357,931 new members by profession of faith, and their total membership was then three and a half million.

But there was a great ingathering of converts even before the New Year of 1858. The Baptists immersed 63,506 believers in 1857, which is double the annual average number for a period of ten years previously. The same denomination baptized 72,080 in the year 1859. Of the three- year total of 227,829 baptisms, it is easy to arrive at the approximate figure of 200,000 for the two years following the outbreak of revival in October 1857. Methodist and Presbyterian and other figures yield the same kind of results, proving that Bishop Candler's estimate of a million converts of the Revival is substantially trustworthy. How shall one account for the fact that the numerical results of the awakening are so often understated? Part of the blame follows the fact that the only contemporary attempt to catalogue the numerical results of the revival was published before the awakening was properly under way. Part of the blame is due to human frailty, for, as the revival produced no great leaders immediately, there were no ardent biographers to search out the achievements of their heroes, as was the case with Wesley and Whitefield and Finney and Moody.

*   *   *   *   *

The Anglican Establishments of England, Wales and Ireland, together with the Nonconformist Episcopalians in Scotland, formed the largest ecclesiastical organization in the United Kingdom in the 1860's.

Anglicans first encountered the Awakening in Ulster in I 859. The Church of Ireland (now disestablished) has always been predominantly evangelical, but a minority of its evangelical leaders has been somewhat exclusive in attitude towards non-Anglican evangelicalism. As a consequence, it is not surprising to find that most Churchmen in Ireland welcomed the I 859 Revival, and some were critical of its extravagant demonstrations and its interdenominational co-operation only.

The background of Scotland, however, was the opposite of the sister Kingdom, as fiercely Reformed Evangelical as the other was Roman Catholic. The Nonconformist Anglicans in opposition to the Presbyterian Establishment represented a more traditionalist and less evangelical Churchmanship, so it is not surprising to note the tone of disapproval of the Revival in the comment of the Bishop of Argyll (Alexander Ewing) that "Revivals certainly create excitement, but not at all of a satisfactory character".

In Wales the bulk of the population adhered to a fiercely Evangelical Dissent, only one-fifth being adherents of the Established Church in Wales. With the figures (20,000 converts) set forth by the Rev. John Venn of Hereford, one may gather from his qualifications the impression that the Welsh Establishment welcomed the Revival only half as enthusiastically as did Dissenting bodies. Nevertheless it is likely that the Church in Wales gained 20,000 or more active communicants, for President David Charles of Trevecca College insisted that the churches of the Welsh Establishment were as powerfully affected as the Dissenting congregations, and this is borne out by other reporters, including Anglican.

In England the Church of England was, in every way, the largest ecclesiastical organization, exceeding in church attendance all other Protestant groups together. The attitude of the Anglican leaders towards the 1859 Revival was as varied as their many schools of thought. This generalization includes the Bishops, who, like the children of Israel in the days of the Judges, did every man that which was right in his own eyes, with similar confusion.

The Bishop of London (Dr. Tait) gave his clergy freedom of action, and twenty-eight of them of note declared that the Revival, in the main, was "the wonderful work of God". Other Bishops, like His Lordship of Carlisle (Dr. Waldegrave), cooperated wholeheartedly in the movement.

The Bishop of Ripon (Dr. Bickersteth), on the other hand, cordially approved an Anglican project for united Revival services in Bradford, but withheld his approval from the interdenominational aspects of the venture. The Anglican clergy and Free Church ministers thereupon arranged an alternating programme of services, with the result that on some Sundays the preachers enjoyed the episcopal blessing as well as Divine approval, while on alternate Sundays the preachers enjoyed Divine approval only.

The High Church Party was generally in opposition to the movement, and the Revivalists in turn regarded the

Tractarians with something akin to horror and revulsion. Besides these overlapping party reactions, there appeared to be a body of indifferent Anglicans who were unreached or unmoved or unhappy about the Revival, which seemed utterly alien to the easy-going religious way of life of their limited experience. Their indifference or opposition seemed due not to positive convictions or doctrines or dogmas, but to lack of them.

"I have always felt," wrote Dr. Eugene Stock in his *Recollections*, "that if our clergy had more heartily welcomed the Revival, its effects within the Church of England would have been much greater."

In contrast, the Baptists co-operated wholeheartedly with the 1859 Revival movement, in Ireland, Scotland, Wales and England. That Baptist opposition or indifference was utterly non-existent would be difficult to prove without reference to the records of every Baptist church in the land. It would be fitter to say that this present research has uncovered not an instance of Baptist opposition to the Awakening. The files of the non-denominational *Revival* weekly, the most comprehensive record of the movement, indicate nothing but whole-hearted co-operation.

Charles Haddon Spurgeon was at the height of his power as a preacher in London whilst the Revival meetings were in full swing. Spurgeon was an unqualified friend of the Awakening, as may be seen clearly from his famous Exeter Hall *Revival Sermon*. So much did he value the Revival that he professed himself alarmed because it appeared to him that many ministers and church members throughout England had slighted its golden opportunities. Spurgeon did not hesitate to claim that his own church had been experiencing incessant Revival for a decade, but, without any diminution of his credit, one may note that the great Metropolitan Tabernacle was built when the crest of the Revival wave had brought Spurgeon's following to a high point in the 1860's.

The building of the Metropolitan Tabernacle was not an isolated event. Dr. W. T. Whitley's work *The Baptists of London* states that the number of Baptist churches founded between 1860 and 1870 and the number surviving from such foundation have never been equalled before or since. He adds that these churches were "as busy as beavers" but "as unsociable as otters". The number of churches built and sustained must be taken as an index of the great ingathering into the Baptist churches of the metropolis. Baptist church sittings in London increased by 33,325 or 60 per cent in the Revival decade.

The whole Baptist denomination in England and Wales, Scotland and Ireland, gained immeasurably from the Awakening. Less than half the Baptist churches of Great Britain were in fellowship with the Union at the turn of the decade. After five years of revival—a revival which stressed unity and co-operation—2,000 of the 2,400 churches adhered to the Union.

From a comparison of the annual reports, it is discovered that there were about 250,000 members in the whole Baptist communion in England and Wales in 1865. Of these 100,000 were the fruits of the Awakening in England and Wales, or approximately 80,000 accessions in England alone. The increase of membership in England, deducting the number of deceased in seven years, is found to be 60,000, a gain of 40 per cent.

The 1859 Assembly of the Congregational Union of England and Wales met at Aberdare at the height of the Welsh Revival and officially recorded its rejoicing over the gracious outpourings. The Congregational

Union of Ireland was formed during the year 1859. The Union meetings in Blackburn, on 11 May 1860, passed a resolution of thanksgiving to God for the blessing brought by the Revival in Ireland.

With the Congregationalists of Ulster, Wales, and Scotland, too, already rejoicing in the movement, the English leaders prayerfully awaited an Awakening and ingathering of less spontaneous effect soon to come. When it came, it added 135,000 members to the Congregational Union of England and Wales, or approximately 90,000 accessions to English churches.

From the commencement of the Revival in Ulster the Methodists profited greatly by the movement in all its phases. In 1859 there were 19,731 people in fellowship with the Irish Methodist Conference. There were 22,860 in full membership in 1860, plus another 2,000 on trial, making a total of about 25,000. That a denomination of 20,000 added 5,000 in a single year underlines the claim of Conference about the Revival, "all our ministers and people entered into it with holy enthusiasm".

Though there were fewer Wesleyan Methodists in Wales than in Ireland, there were comparable gains, 11,859 communicants in 1858 increasing by 4,549 to 16,388 in 1860. Six thousand is the probable number of converts in the whole period.

In England the Wesleyan journal *The Watchman* devoted a leader to the Revival, and prayed that the results of the American movement might be repeated in Britain in 1860. The Prayer was answered in degree.

The Wesleyans apparently added about 20 per cent to their 1858 membership through the influx of converts of the Revival period. Their percentage increase was inferior in quantity to that of the Baptists and the

Congregationalists, neither of whom troubled to pass resolutions of exclusion against free-lance Revivalists. Nevertheless the Awakening of 1859 left a permanent mark upon the ministry of the Wesleyan Methodist Church.

A convert of the Awakening was Hugh Price Hughes, whom Alexander Gammie characterized thus:

"If ever there was a modern Wesley, it was Hugh Price Hughes. He changed not only the outlook of Methodism, but even its atmosphere, and his influence on public life was profound and lasting."

Hurst's *History of Methodism* claims that Methodism received a powerful impetus from the Awakening of the nineteenth century. Known figures and proportionate calculations show the number of converts received by the whole Methodist constituency in England (Wesleyan, Primitive, New Connexion, Free Churches, and Bible Christians) to be 200,000.

The Presbyterian Church in Ireland, an offshoot of the Reformation in Scotland, was the largest denomination in the north of Ireland. One third (454,000 people) of the population of the six counties adhered to it, and in the Province of Ulster there were more than 500,000 Presbyterians. The membership of the Presbyterian Church differed from that of the Methodists or Baptists, for Presbyterianism in Ulster and Scotland is much more of a traditional family religion.

Approximately 16,000 converts were received into fellowship at the first quarterly communion of the Revival period! Complete figures are estimated at 60,000 converts. In 1861, after comprehensive study, the General Assembly declared that "the fruits of the late blessed

Awakening of religion are abiding".

The Presbyterian churches of Great Britain, as in Ireland, received the benefits of the religious Revival very gladly. The Established Church of Scotland in General Assembly recorded its gratitude to God for the blessings brought about by the religious Awakening, expressing cautious watchfulness only about the accompanying manifestations. The General Assembly of the Free Church of Scotland, a more evangelistic and less traditionalistic organization, accepted the Revival without qualification as a blessed fact. The third main body of Presbyterians, the United Presbyterian Synod, was equally happy about the movement.

The number of converts in Scotland amounted to 300,00, the great majority acceding to Presbyterian congregations. Scotland was as powerfully moved by the Revival as were Wales and Ulster, where one-tenth of the Protestant population was reportedly converted, and this ratio applied to Scotland confirms the 300,000 total.

Henry Pickering's *Chief Men Among the Brethren*[1] gives the biographies of a hundred leading lights of the movement. It is significant that thirty-five of the forty-five evangelists or teachers born between 1830 and 1860 were either workers or converts of the 1859 Revival, or both. The residue of ten men eligible by birth may include some who were impressed by the Revival, though this fact is not recorded. Thus about 80 per cent of these Brethren leaders of note were "impressed" in conversion or Christian service by the Awakening.

In England and Wales, by the middle of the nineteenth century, the Society of Friends, or Quakers, had dwindled numerically to less than 15,000 members. No less an

[1]Sometimes designated "Plymouth Brethren".

authority than Dr. Rufus M. Jones, the American church historian, declared that "many Friends were deeply impressed" by the great Revival which began in Ireland in 1859, and that "the Minutes of the Yearly Meeting from 1860 onward reveal a changing outlook on the world and an altered emphasis" in British Quakerism.

With the assessment of the gains of the denominations in the United Kingdom, derived from reliable statistics in the case of the Nonconformists and from speculative estimates in the case of the Established churches, it is possible to present a comprehensive statement of the effect upon the membership of the churches of the Revival of 1859.

There is no doubt that the accessions of converts in Wales exceeded 100,000 seeing that the actual increase in membership in two of the seven years amounted to more than that figure. The number of converts in Ulster and other parts of Ireland exceeded 100,000 also. At least 300,000 converts were won in Scotland. The Nonconformists of England gained at least 400,000 accessions, of whom 370,000 joined the Baptists, Congregationalists and Methodists. The Church of England gain is less reliably estimated at 250,000, though it probably exceeded this figure. The sum total of these figures (1,150,000) exceeds a million. The population of the United Kingdom was approximately 27,000,000 at the time. The adherence of such a proportion of the British population to the evangelical way of life is a factor second only to the evangelical Revival of the eighteenth century in the shaping of the British nation, in the *Pax Britannica* ending in the year 1914.

CHAPTER TEN

CONTEMPORARY CRITICISM

ONE of the most remarkable features of the 1858 Revival of religion in America was the almost unanimous chorus of approval that it received from its contemporaries. It was indeed difficult to find someone who had unkind words to say about the movement.

The secular press received revival news with the utmost enthusiasm. The religious press rejoiced in language of thanksgiving and exultant praise. The opposition came from two widely separated camps, from two schools of thought as far apart as the poles.

In the first instance, there was criticism from Roman Catholic and Anglo-Catholic circles, for the same kind of reason—the Catholic view of the Church. The sight of multitudes flocking to Protestant churches and the report of church memberships being swollen (with only a little increase to Catholicism reported) left "the Pope biting his nails" as a leading Methodist journal described it. The same journal rejoiced that the majority of Churchmen of Anglican affiliation were in sympathy with the movement, the most notable exception being the contemporary New York *Churchman*. In reviewing the revivals, this High-Church paper[1] bewailed the fact that the converts of the revivals were entering the sects and not the true Church.

Critics were unable to lay the charge of fanaticism,

[1] Now Liberal.

or hysteria, or any of the favourite accusations against revivals. So they contented themselves with declaring that a revival which filled other churches, but not their own, could not be of Divine origin. Their criticism received very little attention from either secular or religious press, and no controversy was raised by their observations. The evangelical people, Anglican and others, were so well satisfied with the fruits of the revival that they felt generously sorry for the unfortunate ecclesiastics who, though not really believing in that kind of fruit, found their mouths watering in vain.

On the other hand, the *Abend Zeitung* (organ of the School of German Rationalists) was torn between desires to explain the revival and to depreciate it. It declared:

"Germans who come to America, be they freethinkers or believers in God, Protestants or Catholics, will find little relief in their minds of religion in the manner exhibited by the American people. There is a closer relationship between the German Rationalists and the extreme German Pietists, than there is between either of these and any of the religious sects in America... the serious and almost grotesque manner in which the requests for prayer for the soul of ex-Alderman Smith, the pugilist Miller, the Millionaire Brown, or the widow Black, are complied with, has a very ridiculous appearance."

The strongest attack upon the Revival came from another rationalist source, this time one within the pale of organized religion, the Reverend Theodore Parker of Boston. Theodore Parker, described as an American theologian of rationalist views and one of the brightest intellects of his day, had already shocked his Unitarian confrères with his advanced views. At one time, the

Unitarian ministry wanted to expel him, but did not; and he refused to resign, for he felt strongly that as a Unitarian minister he was free to express himself. So Mr. Parker continued to shock even Boston with extreme statements, such as his opinion that in all probability there would be new Christs manifested in generations to come.

It appears from one of Mr. Parker's sermons that he attended one of the union prayer-meetings in Boston, and indeed offered a prayer there. Whereupon, some zealous conservative rose to draw attention to the fact that the man who had just prayed was really outside the fold, and proceeded to pray earnestly for Theodore Parker's conversion. This unfortunate incident riled the rationalist theologian beyond measure. Soon his bitter words were in the leading papers of the country, causing one to remark that "Mr. Parker has evidently been sorely bruised by the hard hits of the revivalists, not to say by their prayers". Many ardent souls tried hard to convert Theodore Parker personally, but they wasted their sweetness on the desert air, leaving their victim decidedly agitated.

The *Boston Courier* of April 5, 1858, carried a lengthy report of Mr. Parker's sermon on "False and True Revival". Said he:

"In this city, in March 1858, in a meeting-house, a Saturday afternoon, we find honest and respectable men and women met together for prayer and conference; most exciting speeches are made; exciting stories are told; fanatical prayers are put up; a part of the assembly seems beside themselves and out of their minds; they say, 'The Lord is in Chicago and a great revival is going on there; the Lord is in Boston and He has poured out His Spirit here'."

Such remarks, according to Mr. Parker, would show that the people making them were somewhat unbalanced mentally. He went on to pour out his vials of wrath upon Park Street Church, which was the antithesis of all that he stood for theologically. In a more general way, he thought that the Revival was demonstrating that the people could not get enough of preaching, the poorer the article (in his opinion) the more they wanted of it. Some Unitarian churches had been revived, but in Mr. Parker's judgment "as well might we expect to produce fire by friction of ice blocks, as to expect a revival among the Unitarians".

Mr. Parker's theory of the Revival was very simple— the whole thing had been very skilfully got up...

"There are a hundred men in every congregation superior in talent and learning to their pastor, and can best him in argument or reasoning. So the minister tries to scare men into belief of his doctrine and membership in his church."

Parker thought that some good had been done, but averred that the revivalists were really presenting a hideous form of Deity. He described the part played in the Revival by the newspapers, saying that if the same newspapers could turn a penny, they cared not where it came from, whether from a revival or an adultery.

The evangelicals of Boston redoubled their prayers for Mr. Parker's conversion, but with less assurance of fulfilment. They sought to defend evangelical principles, and to attack rationalism and its advocate. A week later, the press commented that "Theodore Parker is determined that the blows which have fallen on his heterodoxy shall not go unreturned". He preached another sermon, on "True Revivals"; and it was summarized in the press thus:

"Park Street Church, Pro-Slavery, the Democrats, the President, Prayer Meetings, and Prayer itself received the benefits of Mr. Parker's deepest denunciation; and Mormonism, Spiritualism, and Emersonianism were commended equally without stint."

He was certainly a bold man to commend the Mormons at a time when the whole country was scandalized by their polygamous marriages and their treatment of emigrants to the West; but Mormonism had "something mankind wants", just as Spiritualism was "a desire for communion with God".

Boston was the only place, apparently, where the Revival stirred up violent controversy. And the work of grace in Boston was less in extent than in the other larger cities. Perhaps if the zealous believer had shown a kinder spirit towards Theodore Parker, his obvious early interest in the Revival might have blossomed into a spiritual experience.

As the Awakening of 1858 occurred in the modern newspaper age, its course was bound to be affected by the attitudes that the Press generally took to the movement. That the religious press should support the Revival is not at all surprising, but the overwhelming enthusiasm of the secular press is wholly astounding. The historian cannot escape the conclusion that the secular press was the Revival's greatest earthly ally.

The *Presbyterian Magazine* voiced its wonder at the phenomenon thus:

"Since the first settlement of our country, no religious movement has attracted more attention than the present. As might be expected, the religious press has chronicled numerous incidents connected with this work. But, what has seldom occurred before, the secular newspapers have also appropriated a portion of their columns almost daily, for two or three months, in giving detailed notices of prayer-meetings in our large cities and various other particulars concerning the movement throughout our whole country."

The beginning of the alliance between the Revival and the Press is seen in the modest diary of Jeremiah Lanphier, who, on January 5, 1858, "called with some of the editors of the daily papers in regard to having some of the incidents, which occur in the prayer-meetings, inserted in them". One can almost imagine that first call of the quiet-spoken lay-worker upon the busy editor of a New York paper. The editor would have been engrossed in his daily chores, but the devout missioner undoubtedly gained a hearing by his sincere importunity. No doubt the editor scratched his head while debating with himself whether or not to give space to a prayer-meeting—*a prayer-meeting*! What would his rival editors think! Upon second thoughts, the editor must have decided that religion was what was needed in the day of crisis so either he or one of his staff paid a visit to the meetings in question, just to see.

At any rate, the researchist begins thumbing the dusty files of an American newspaper of 1858, anxiously looking for a mention of the Awakening. In January, odd notices occurred in papers from Atlantic to Mississippi, but they were not couched in extraordinary language. In February, the big New York dailies opened their columns to what was happening in their midst, and the trickle of news became a rivulet, swelling to a flood within the space of weeks. Soon the historian suffers from writer's cramp trying to take notes from the yellowing pages of the press; and he is finally forced to make little selections from the multitude of paragraphs and columns dealing with the Revival.

By March, 1858, the secular press was giving whole columns to intelligence of the Awakening. Heavy headlines, *The Hour of Prayer*, *The Revivals*, *The Great Awakenings*, *The Religious Awakening*, *The Religious Movement*, and the like, literally loaded the printed page. Why did the editors of the various papers give such space to a purely religious movement? There are two good reasons. It is obvious that the Revival was engrossing the whole nation, and that the people demanded revival news. When a Western editor saw a column generously devoted to religion in a New York contemporary, he saw the trend and found that the example was good. Another good reason is found in the startling effect of the Revival upon the editors and journalists themselves. Often the historian, in scanning a particular journal, says to himself at a certain point "this is where the editor became converted himself!"

The news of the Revival displaced other news, and held premier place for several months. In ordinary times the most successful religious movement rated a bare mention in the national papers, so overwhelmed is religious news by the welter of political, international, social, market, and sports intelligence, not to mention crime and divorce. While life in 1858 was not as complex as life three generations later, it should be noted that the Awakening had as its rivals such topics as the Indian Mutiny, which stirred Americans to sympathy with their massacred cousins in India, the Slavery Question, which was causing bloody rioting and fighting in many places and was soon to rend the nation in twain, and the Financial

Depression, which scared people everywhere.

The decline in the amount of space given the Awakening must not be thought of as paralleling a decline in the strength of the Revival. It was a natural result, for when the Revival got under way, it became so commonplace that it was no longer regarded as startling news. Instead of astounding instances, editors began featuring summaries of results. The Revival was an accepted fact in American life.

A paragraph from the Cincinnati *Daily Commercial* is illuminating:

"The advertising columns of newspapers exhibit signs of the times. In one of yesterday's papers, we noticed an advertisement notifying the public that 'Boarding can be had in a Christian family.' Another asserted that 'A young man, a professing Christian, desires a situation'!"

The secular press became the instrument of revival in no small way. A pastor wrote to the editor of one of the newspapers, saying: "The glorious summary, with the editorial remarks on the *Great Revivals* in your paper of the 4th instant, stirred my soul so powerfully that I felt that something must be done in our village; and I have called on the other ministers, and we have started a meeting, and the dews are falling on us."

A contemporary writer used the following description of the part played by the American press in the Awakening:

"The Press, which speaks in the ear of millions, is taken possession of by the Spirit, willing or unwilling, to proclaim His wonders, and go everywhere preaching the word, in its most impressive, its living forms and examples... a new thing, and, under God, a mighty thing

in the religious world. The barest statement in figures...
is more eloquent of divine love than the voice of an
apostle."

Some organs of the British press, claiming a higher
standard of journalistic integrity, stooped lower in their
treatment of the I 859 Revival, these attacks being not
merely due to misunderstanding and misinformation.
[Footnote: The British press generally treated Moody
and Sankey with vitriolic scorn, but their 285 meetings
in London were attended by an aggregate of 2,500,000
people.]

For example, the Belfast *Northern Whig*, which
disliked the Revival upon religious grounds (it was of
Unitarian background), attacked the movement in the
pettiest possible ways. Lest this example be attributed to
Irish zeal for combat in the journalistic field one must
point out that the same sort of thing was perpetrated
(with as feeble justification) by *The Times* of London in
attributing to the Revival a propensity for driving people
mad, a theme which its editors greatly stressed in spite of
all evidence to the contrary.

Throughout the news-worthy period of the Ulster
Revival *The Times* adopted an attitude of opposition to
the movement, leaving no possible criticism unsaid. It
consistently played up all that the enemies of the Revival
had to say, and consistently ignored or played down or
contradicted everything that the friends of the Revival
claimed.

Dr. G. M. Trevelyan comments on the unfortunate
influence of *The Times* of that very period thus:

"So little was America known to the readers of *The
Times* that, when the great newspaper declared pontifically

that Yankees were cowards and that slavery was not an issue in the struggle, Belgravia and its dependencies believed what they read."

It is easy to paraphrase that assessment and add- so little did the readers of *The Times* know of Spiritual Awakening that, when the great newspaper decided pontifically that the Revival was all fanaticism, doing harm instead of good, anti-evangelicals, secular and religious, believed what they read and acted accordingly.

Charles Dickens made reference to the Ulster Awakening in his writings. The novelist proclaimed the outbreak of hysteria and denied the reports of moral improvement by quoting Belfast statistics, "those fatal figures, those unenthusiastic, disbelieving, obstinate statistics, to destroy all these beautiful assertions".

The Rev. Franklin Bewley, Episcopal clergyman of Tullylish, County Down, retorted:

"I was never so shocked as with the gross falsehood of *The Times* that the result of the movement has been to fill the streets of Belfast with prostitutes and drunken revellers. Never was there a more manifest distortion of facts."

Nevertheless, the Mayor of Belfast (himself a friend of the Revival) admitted that there was an increase in the number of cases brought before the magistrates in the city of Belfast. In 1858 there were 2,539 cases of drunkenness: in 1859, 3,112, an increase of 573. Of this increase Professor Gibson stated:

"If it had been asserted by the advocates of the religious movement that every individual of the 120,000 or 130,000 inhabitants of Belfast had been brought under the influence of the Revival, these statistics of drunkenness might be legitimately appealed to in the case. But it is a fact which admits of no dispute that *no person has, during the year in question, been brought before the police court of Belfast, on a charge of drunkenness, who has ever been brought under religious influences."*

Whether the explanation of the increase of drunkenness in Belfast is legitimate or otherwise will continue to be a matter of controversy. *The Times* emphasized the apparently unfavourable statistics again on March 28, 1860, but the religious press retorted that none of the inebriates was a convert of the Revival.

The British Standard pointed out that in the county of Derry there were 100,000 Presbyterians, but not one drunken person called himself a Presbyterian, adding that the question did not turn upon the number of cases, but upon their religious profession.

In an endeavour to settle this controversy, the following authoritative figures have been secured:

CRIMINAL CONVICTIONS IN THE SIX COUNTIES, 1855-61

	1855	1856	1857	1858	1859	1860	1861
Antrim	254	123	146	129	104	66	79
Armagh	125	119	69	100	84	133	115
Derry	96	90	78	85	60	42	73
Down	163	147	153	130	104	82	111
Fermanagh	70	80	54	101	53	48	119
Tyrone	181	195	128	91	70	85	96
	889	754	628	636	475	456	593

These statistics for the six counties seem to show that the period of the Revival produced a considerable decrease in crime.

The Belfast News Letter reported decreased drunkenness and depravity as a result of the Revival, and quoted a Belfast police constable as averring that he had not seen a drunken person for weeks; the former average of convictions being twenty-one monthly, but only sixteen occurring in April, four in May and none in June or July, in his district.

At the Ballymena Quarter-Sessions, April 1860, His Worship congratulated the community that there was not a single case of indictment upon the record. At the Quarter-Sessions in Coleraine, April 1860, the judge congratulated the jury that there was only one new case to be considered, a very unimportant one. At the Quarter-Sessions in Belfast, April 1860, there were only three cases, all of them trifling in character. At the Quarter-Sessions in Londonderry, April 1860, there was no criminal business at all, and His Worship was presented with a pair of white gloves. At the Quarter-Sessions in Down, April 1860, there were no prisoners appearing on the calendar. Comment is superfluous.

Another charge made by the *Northern Whig* against the movement was that it increased insanity. Both Dr. Gibson and Dr. Weir exploded the local figures given by the Whig conclusively. Neither had access to the comprehensive figures based upon the Inspector of Asylums Reports, which showed that, in spite of a widening definition (in the years 1851-61), the total number of insane in asylums and under restraint in Ireland in 1859 was 11,218 as compared with 14,141 two years earlier and 16,732 two years later.

The religious professions of lunatics in Ulster in 1861 showed that 49 per cent were Protestants and 50.5 per cent Roman Catholics, these being the exact percentages of Protestants and Roman Catholics in the general Ulster population. This fact demonstrates how little religious belief had to do with the incidence of insanity, and makes superfluous in this case the argument of Dr. Gibson that the Crusades and the Reformation and all great movements increased insanity.

So often was the charge reiterated by the enemies of the Revival that there was an increase of sexual immorality that the opinion persists in Ulster to this day. Reference has been made already to Mr. Nelson's opinions, and those of the *Northern Whig*, *The Times*, Charles Dickens and others willing to accept them. There is plenty of local evidence to the contrary.

Rev. John Baillie was startled to learn of a prayer-meeting being held by the converted inmates of a house of ill-fame. Benjamin Scott, Chamberlain of the City of London, reported that the Ulster Penitentiary for the Reform of Fallen Women was in great need of funds and space to take care of the influx of converted prostitutes seeking rehabilitation. Dr. Hugh Hanna, noting that Belfast was infected as elsewhere by the great social evil, declared that the movement had entered into the haunts of its worst wickedness, bringing many a Magdalene to the feet of Christ and enabling ministers to get a congregation of attentive and tearful listeners in such places. In a later letter Dr. Hanna revealed that certain prostitutes confessed that they were first made to consider an amended life by the falling off in business. The Rev. John Venn of Hereford quoted a Belfast policeman who saw a body of fourteen prostitutes making their way to a

House of Refuge, the result of a visit to a prayer-meeting. Similar instances could be multiplied.

Most of these instances concerned the reform of professional harlots, and not the incidence of occasional promiscuity with its outcome, illegitimacy. The only possible check upon the occurrence of non-professional immorality would have been the Registrar-General's summary of illegitimate births. Alas, in Ireland, compulsory registration of births and deaths was begun in 1864, too late for reference value.

In this connection the illegitimacy figures for Scotland may be of value, for the people there were racially, temperamentally and denominationally akin to Ulster folk, and the Revival movement followed the same pattern of expression. In all Scotland, the Registrar-General's figures show a tiny fractional rise in illegitimacy year by year, except in 1860, when the effects of the Awakening would be noticed, when the figure of illegitimacy per cent remained stationary—1859, 9.0 per cent; 1860, 9.0 per cent; 1861, 9.2 per cent; 1862, 9.5 per cent.

It may be that the excitement of the times in Ulster provided increased temptation for young people unaware of the effect of the stirring of the emotions upon the urge for sex-expression: but the charge of increased illegitimacy is unproved and appears unlikely, even though there may have been an increase in certain parishes.

CHAPTER ELEVEN

CHRISTIAN ACTION

A S PRAYER, the great method of the Awakening of 1858, became uniquely demonstrated for all generations, so too the rise of the laity as the instrument of the movement was striking.

This point has not been missed by historians. Bishop Warren Candler states:

"The working forces of the churches were immeasurably increased. The revival of 1858 inaugurated in some sense the era of lay work in American Christianity. Wesley's system of class leaders, exhorters, and local preachers had done much at an early date in the same direction, but now the layman's day fully dawned on all the churches. No new doctrine was brought forward, but a new agency was brought to bear in spreading the old truth through the efforts of men who, if they could not interpret the scriptures with precision or train souls to perfection, could at least help inquiring sinners to find the Lord by relating how they themselves had found Him. Since Christianity is a religion of experience, this lay element was a power in the Apostolic Church, of whom were St. Stephen and St. Luke. But it dropped out of the Church when Christianity, ceasing to be an experience, was practiced only as a pompous system of priest-craft or taught as an abtuse philosophy of religion. It now returned in the regeneration of a nation."

Beardsley indulges in a similar expression of sentiment, saying:

"This divine visitation, providential in its character, was emphatically a lay revival. There was no evangelist of national reputation, no minister, however influential, to whom credit could be given for this mighty work of grace, even as the indirect instrument of its accomplishment. The revival was carried on independently of the ministry and almost without their aid. The ministry were not ignored, nor was there in any sense an opposition to them. They carried on their regular services, but to greatly increased congregations, which were the immediate fruits of the revival, and by their preaching and prayers they gave encouragement to the work and co-operated with it. The laity were especially active. The movement commenced with the efforts of a layman, it enlisted the sympathies and energies of other laymen throughout the country, and was carried on chiefly through their instrumentality."

In the first place, most of the organizers of the daily union prayer-meetings were businessmen. The Fulton Street meeting was commenced by a lay-worker. The John Street meeting was begun and sustained by young businessmen. The Burton's Theatre meeting was launched by down-town merchants. The Jayne's Hall service in Philadelphia was maintained by businessmen. And so on, all over the country.

Another significant lay development was the way in which meetings were provided by Christian men for their fellows in industry and the professions. For example, the policemen of the Seventeenth Ward in New York City notified their Captain, Hartt, that they desired to have a religious meeting for their mutual benefit. Stanton Street

Baptist Church was appointed as the place for assembly, and by 2.30 p.m. that day, the church was crowded, half by police in uniform and half by the families and friends. That was Monday, March 29, 1858. On April 7, the church was host to another meeting of policemen, at which police and policemen's wives testified of saving grace. The example of this first venture among police was soon being copied elsewhere.

Likewise, the Firemen of the City were the objects of special efforts. Under the leadership of Y.M.C.A. zealots, a mass meeting was arranged at the Academy of Music, where "the capacious building was never more crowded", "every seat was taken", "all the standing room in the aisles and doorways was densely packed, and hundreds were unable to obtain an entrance". In Philadelphia thirty-eight companies of firemen sent delegates to divine worship, their grand total being 1,779 attending one meeting in National Hall.

Paralleling this movement for large assemblies of various groups in business life, the Awakening provoked a host of smaller meetings held in the stores and counting-houses of all sorts of commercial houses. The workers in a certain concern, or the manager of a store, or an outsider, would propose a daily meeting on the premises—and so it was! The idea spread throughout the length and breadth of the land.

A typical product of the Awakening was Dwight L. Moody, whose experiences in the Chicago revival of religion in 1858 and 1859 shaped him and his ministry as did no other force. Truly Beardsley comments:

"The revival, moreover, served as a great training school for laymen, and brought to light the abilities of such men as D. L. Moody, who has left a lasting impress upon the history of American Christianity."

The 1858 movement left a powerful mark in the ministry of D. L. Moody. For instance, when he crossed to Great Britain, one of his first ideas in every great city was to launch a permanent noonday daily union prayer-meeting. The writer has often attended the meeting begun by D. L. Moody in Glasgow, meeting week after week, and organized on the lines set out in the movement of 1858. Again, Moody made a point of trying to reach various groups of people in all his great campaigns. Again, the Y.M.CA., which backed the 1858 Revival wholeheartedly, became Moody's favourite organization, and undoubtedly the work of that body in the 1858 revival commended itself to Moody's practical mind. Again, Moody's greatest success was in his ability to set laymen to work in Christian activity. The great Bible School movement is testimony of this. Where did it begin? Moody was convinced of the place of the laity in 1858.

As a natural corollary of the movement of the laity, the movement towards practical interdenominational unity developed rapidly. Most lay movements are interdenominational, and most revivals of religion are interdenominational as well. In the Awakening of 1858, the various denominations were so busy trying to cater for the influx of new members that there was no room for sectarian jealousy. With scarcely an exception, the churches were working as one man. Arminian and Calvinist ignored their differences; Baptists and Paedobaptists were blessed together; and everything was lovely, almost too good to be true. By common consent, doctrinal controversies were left alone, and the idea worked well. At last the world was able to say, without irony, "Behold, how these Christians love one another!"

The fruits of the rise of the laity and its consequent promotion of interdenominational fellowship were better seen in the Moody and Sankey revivals, and in the great interdenominational agencies and fellowships supported by Moody. The 1858 Awakening in America was noted for its Home Mission work. The revivals of a score of years later were noted for their emphasis on Foreign Missions. The regeneration of Foreign Missionary Interest would have come earlier had it not been for the slavery issue and the Civil War of 1861-5. In 1858, there were many calls for a revival of missionary interest. *The Baptist Missionary Magazine* of October 1858 asked:

"Many of the churches of America have been recently blessed as never before... The question now arises— what ought to be the effect of this great revival on the missionary cause?"

Before the answer could come, the fratricidal war between the States drained the nation's energy and provided the churches with a crusade. The oppressed at home were liberated first. In the absence of Civil War in Britain, there was immediate flowering of the Awakening in the revival of many existing organizations and the creation of new ones. The Revival brought a flood of blessing down the old channels and broke through obstacles to form new rivers of Christian enterprise.

The British and Foreign Bible Society had celebrated its Jubilee in 1854. Five years later the Awakening brought a host of helpers to the noble band of workers in that great enterprise. Historians of the Bible Societies give little credit to the cause of the sudden expansion of the 1860's, but they record the effects. For example, the

1859 Revival first affected Ulster. Within the year the Hibernian Bible Society ceased to be an auxiliary which got help from the parent Society instead of giving help. To this day the people of Ulster have remained a Bible-loving community, whose knowledge of the Scriptures is second to no comparable community in the world. The 1859-60 Awakening in Scotland produced much the same sort of results in the northern kingdom. In 1861 the National Bible Society of Scotland was established and began to express the energetic efforts of the revived Scottish churches to promote the rapid evangelization of the world. Progress was likewise made in the Principality of Wales, under the leadership of the energetic and consecrated secretary, Dr. Phillips. The 1860's were years of expansion for the Welsh Bible auxiliaries, for Revival had given the Welsh Christians, mature and immature, a love for the Bible in their mother tongue.

G. M. Trevelyan has noted the effect of the Evangelical Revival of the eighteenth century upon the social life of Britain. Of the evangelicals, he says "Humanitarian activity was the characteristic form in which their religious piety expressed itself". The Evangelical Awakening of the nineteenth century, primarily evangelistic, developed a social conscience as liberal as its theology was conservative. Dr. Trevelyan (designating the Salvation Army as "the last great evangelical Revival" instead of as a development of it) notes that this nineteenth-century Revival "brought the enthusiasm of 'conversion', after Wesley's original fashion, to the army of the homeless and unfed, to the drunkard, the criminal and the harlot" regarding "social work and care for the material conditions of the poor and outcast as being an essential part of the Christian mission to the souls of men and women". These tributes belong to the 1859 Revival as a whole.

One of the first effects of the Awakening of 1859 was the creation of a new and intense sympathy with the poor and suffering. "God," urged Lord Shaftesbury, "has not ordained that in a Christian country there should be an overwhelming mass of foul, helpless poverty." Lord Shaftesbury, of course, had been active long before the Revival, but with the 1859 movement a new day dawned and a Revival School of Christian Philanthropists arose, endeavouring to go straight to the heart of the slums with a practical Samaritanism, yet always ready to co-operate in all wise legislative improvements. So, as the Revivals intensified the fervour of belief, denominational schemes, organizations, places of worship, were multiplied, and numberless philanthropic institutions—homes, asylums, refuges, brigades, schools—were founded in all parts of the country.

George E. Morgan, M.A., biographer of his father, R. C. Morgan, founder of *The Christian*, sums up the effects of the Revival of 1859 upon Home Missions thus:

"... surveying the vast growth of Home Missions, the conviction gains force that the period following the Revival of 1859 was one of the most fruitful in the annals of Christianity in this country; and also that in these later days, when so many criticize and scepticize about Revival, it cannot be too strongly emphasized that the *entire Home Mission Movement was not only inaugurated and manned, but also financed,* by Revival converts and sympathizers."

The conclusions emphasized by Mr. Morgan's own italics happily can be well substantiated.

During the Revival period in Dublin several members of a brilliant family named Barnardo professed to accept Christ as Saviour in the Metropolitan Hall meetings. Two of the Barnardo brothers endeavoured to persuade their younger brother Tom, but he scoffed. Nevertheless he attended the meetings and witnessed striking demonstrations of spiritual power. These he explained away as emotional hysteria and psychological phenomena, but, in spite of his subtle arguments, he was set to thinking. Later, Tom Barnardo attended a smaller meeting in the home of a devout Christian named William Fry. He remained cynical, in his own words "just as cheeky" as a young fellow could be. But an address by John Hambledon in the same place some weeks later caused him such conviction that long after midnight he sought, in great distress and with many tears, his brothers' help. So he was converted on May 26, 1862. Tom Barnardo became attached to a Bible-class run by Grattan Guinness, who invited young Hudson Taylor to address the company on the needs of China. There young Barnardo heard the call to missionary service and volunteered to go, but tragic discoveries in the dismal East End of London led him into his life-work, one of the greatest philanthropic tasks of the past hundred years, the founding of Dr. Barnardo's Homes, the world's largest orphanage.

Needless to say, the Sunday-schools of Britain received a great influx of children from the homes of revived Christians and newly won converts. In August 1859 the editor of The Revival published a report entitled *Effects of the Revival on Sunday-schools*, telling of a spirit of inquiry among both parents and children in Ireland. The committee of the Sunday-school Society for Ireland made it clear that:

"Education is now become the principal object

of concern amongst the uneducated class in this neighbourhood (County Antrim), both of old and young. The present Revival has created a thirsting desire for the Word of God, and it is their continual and increasing study to learn to read it for themselves. The spirit of inquiry is so great, that we have been induced to open the school two evenings during the week, for the purpose of communicating instruction."

From that time onwards the Awakening began to fill the Sunday-schools of the three kingdoms with children eager to learn their spiritual lessons. Not only in the spontaneous Revival areas of Ulster, Scotland and Wales, but in England there was an upsurge of attendance. The conversions of thousands of senior scholars in Newcastle-on-Tyne has been already noted. The statistics of one denomination, covering seven years, showed a more than 33 per cent increase of Sunday-school attendances, and other denominations reported more than 50 per cent. Not only was there an increase of numbers of children under instruction, but the phenomena of child-conversion occurred in so many parts of the country as to be considered usual.

The 1859 Awakening created new agencies for the evangelization of the children. An American student, Edward Payson Hammond, studying theology in Scotland, was caught up by the Revival movement in Dumfries and elsewhere. His greatest contribution to the religious life of Great Britain was his great emphasis upon *child conversion*. Hammond used what were then considered novel methods to interest juveniles, and set T. B. Bishop and Josiah Spiers afire with the idea of *child evangelism*, and the result of their application of his principles to their problems was the foundation of the Children's Special

Service Mission (C.S.S.M.), an evangelistic agency whose effect in so many walks of life cannot be overestimated. The very title of the society bears the mark of the 1860 crop of evangelical agencies.

The effects of the Awakening among university students has already been noted in the chapter mentioning Oxford and Cambridge. The fast-growing, conservative Inter-Varsity Christian Fellowship of this present generation may be traced back to the 1859 Revival, the theology of which it still maintains. For a while the Christian Union groups participated in a much later upsurge of student Christian activity, but parted company when the sister organization became liberalized in policy and theology.

The Young Men's Christian Associations were already in existence when the Great Awakening began. Out of the Revival of 1858 came the introduction of the Y.M.C.A. to American cities, and the flowering of the movement in the United States. The influx of converted young men into Christian churches found an outlet in the evangelistic activities of the early Y.M.CA. The editor of *The Revival*, in the journal's second issue, pointed out:

"It does not necessarily follow that because the Young Men's Christian Association has been so blessed in the American Revival, the same must be the case in this country. There might be an attempt at imitation followed by humiliating failure. But we think it will not be so. Our connexion with the Association is, indeed, but of recent date, but we have seen enough to lead us to expect God's blessing upon it in a very marked manner when His time is come."

R. C Morgan's prophecy was well fulfilled. From the

beginning of the Awakening in Britain the Y.M.C.A. not only shared in the in-gathering, but often sponsored the meetings which brought Christians together for united prayer and united evangelism. A conference of provincial and metropolitan delegates met in London at the outbreak of the Revival, and reiterated an early principle of the Y.M.C.A. binding upon all branches—*decided and well-authenticated conversion to God* as the requirement for membership. From that time forward, the Y.M.C.A. grew with the Revival. The effect of the 1858-9 Revivals upon the Y.M.C.A. is scarcely mentioned in standard histories on the subject. The year 1864, however, is officially recognized as "the turning point of the Y.M.C.A.", "the beginning of certain success". In 1864 the Edinburgh Conference of the Y.M.C.A. laid the foundations of the modern Y.M.C.A., with a liberal provision for the all-round requirements of young men. The revived Youth leaders of the 1860s had an excellent balance of spiritual and social aims.

In the early months of the Revival in London an attempt was made to evangelize and reclaim the prostitutes who frequented the drinking-dens and dancing-rooms and streets of the West End. At the outset many fallen girls burst into tears when addressed by the saintly Baptist Noel, who talked very tenderly to them. The sponsors of the work took a score of penitents to Houses of Refuge, such as the Homes for Friendless and Fallen Women. The enterprise of the rescue workers was shown in their meetings for foreign-born prostitutes, who had the Gospel preached to them in their own tongue. R. C. Morgan, editor of *The Revival*, took a great interest in this work of mercy, hence the columns of his paper were always open for reports of the Midnight Meeting Movement, as it was called. The Midnight Meeting

Movement spread to the other cities of Britain. Reports of the rescue work are too numerous to be chronicled, but it is said that 1,000 women were rescued within a year. Stalwarts, such as Mrs. Josephine Butler, took up the fight against social evils. Mrs. Butler, in spite of bitter and brutal opposition, campaigned heroically for the repeal of licensing of vice. Within eight years of the outbreak of the Revival Christian opinion had been sufficiently mobilized to form a *National Association for Repeal* of the obnoxious Government patronage of prostitution. Eight years later more than 2,000,000 signatures were presented in petition to Parliament. Another eight years of struggle ensued before the Criminal Law Amendment Bill of 1885 was passed.

The most significant and the most fascinating home development of the 1859 Awakening was the birth of the Salvation Army. The achievements of William and Catherine Booth as evangelists during the seven years of the Revival have already been described in great detail. Booth's experiences in Cornwall taught him the connection between holiness of Christian living and successful evangelism, for he preached one to achieve the other. His experience in the Black Country Revivals taught him that the masses could be most successfully reached by their own kind bearing witness. His frustration at the hands of unsympathetic denominational directors must have determined him to shape an organization of his own. He was an inter-denominationalist, yet his Arminian convictions were strong; and so his brain-child, the Salvation Army, became inter-denominational in the support it commanded from all sorts of Christians, yet denominational enough to be considered a convinced Arminian fellowship, more Wesleyan than the modern Methodists.

Colonel Robert Sandall's *History of the Salvation Army* has completely upset the ideas of the average informed Salvationist about the birth of the movement. Before the Second World War few Salvation Army officers were aware of any connection between the 1859 Revival and the founding of their movement. Colonel Sandall's conclusions are well substantiated. In the New Year of 1861 a conference was called in the Sussex Hall in Leadenhall Street in the City of London to consider the appalling need of the East End. There the Rev. Baptist Noel predicted that a far reaching work was about to begin, and so the East London Special Services Committee began its modest operations. Six months later William Booth visited London friends to seek employment in some Home Mission activity, and was put into contact with the leaders of the East London committee. They invited him to become their evangelist, but four years of successful Revivalism elsewhere intervened before Booth accepted their invitation. Into this opportunity for service William Booth poured his passion for soul-winning and his great experience of ministry in the Revival. The committee's work soon became the Christian Revival Association; then the East London Christian Mission; then, as the efforts were extended, the Christian Mission, which was finally renamed the Salvation Army. The Salvation Army arose as a permanent expression of the 1859 Revival in its double ministry of evangelism and social uplift. Most of its activities to-day are those which were already begun by other workers of the Awakening—evangelism, indoor and outdoor, mission to fallen women, to criminals, social welfare work, missionary enterprise. Whilst the Salvation Army bears the indelible stamp of the personalities of William and Catherine Booth, it was cast by them in the mould of the 1859 Revival.

In the centenary sketch of the World's Evangelical Alliance, *Goodly Fellowship*, Dr. J. W. Ewing makes a passing reference to the 1859 Revival, but does not describe the part which the Evangelical Alliance played in the commencement and extension of the remarkable Awakening, a part of great importance, for the Evangelical Alliance not only prepared the ground for the seed of co-operation between Christians of various loyalties, but once the plant had sprung up, watered it most thoroughly.

When in 1846 the Evangelical Alliance was founded to enable Christians of all nations to realize in themselves and to manifest to others the living and essential union which unites all believers in the fellowship of Christ, a score of distinguished leaders of the Church Universal attended the sessions. The majority of them are recognizable as promoters of the 1859 Awakening. Far more than in personalities, the Evangelical Alliance influenced the 1859 Awakening by its principles. One was its testimony to the unity of all believers in Christ, for it held, as did the early Brethren, that as soon as a sinner accepted Christ as Saviour he became one with all the members of the Body of Christ throughout the earth. Another was its doctrinal basis, a matter reserved for further treatment. It is noteworthy that the first outbreak of extraordinary Revival in England, the Newcastle-on-Tyne movement in 1859, gave rise to such a happy degree of Christian co-operation that the work was designated "the Evangelical Alliance Revival".

Perhaps the greatest contribution of the Evangelical Alliance to the 1859 Revival was its programme of prayer. In 1860 the group of missionaries at Ludhiana in India appealed to the Alliance to extend their call to prayer to all the world. The Evangelical Alliance did so, making the second week of January 1860 a Universal Week of Prayer. The response was phenomenal. In the areas where the fruits of Revival had already been harvested there was a further crop; where the ground was prepared, immediate manifestations of Revival sprang up; and where the ground was hard, it was raked and watered by praying Christians for one, two or more years until their prayers were answered in the evangelistic phase of the Awakening. "The Universal Week of Prayer" has continued to this day, through the medium of about 100 languages.

In 1856 a leader of the Evangelical Alliance (Dr. Steane) urged its members to join in the preliminary special services for the masses being carried on in the Exeter Hall, and called for similar efforts wherever possible. In the 1860s the aggregate attendance at special services in London alone exceeded 1,000,000 a season, or 50,000 a Sunday. The special services were carried on by the pro- Revival Christian leaders, on an Evangelical Alliance basis of cooperation. There seems no doubt that the whole of the 1859 Revival movement was one great unofficial Evangelical Alliance in itself. The operation did not cease with the Revival. The principles of Christian union put forth by the Evangelical Alliance in 1846, and practised on a world-wide scale in the Awakening of 1858, 1859 and the 1860s, conditioned Christians the world over for the great inter-denominational Councils of the twentieth century.

The Keswick Convention Movement for the Deepening of the Spiritual Life, an evangelical movement with a truly world-wide influence, budded at gatherings in London, Oxford and Brighton in 1873-4-5, and blossomed into early maturity at the Derwentwater resort in 1875; but the seed was sown in the great Revival of 1858-60 in the English-speaking world.

In 1860 an American Christian under Revival influence published a book entitled *The Higher Christian Life* which made a profound impression upon many lives. That year was also the year of Evan Hopkins' spiritual rebirth, and it was not long before a copy of Dr. Boardman's treatise found its way into the hands of Evan Hopkins, who was then engaged in engrossing Revival ministry, and had not reached the period when time for reflection and retrospect would lead him into a deeper blessing. On May 29, 1875, 7,000 people attended meetings at Brighton. And wholeheartedly backing the Convention with the prayers of 8,000 followers was Dwight L. Moody, then closing his gigantic Gospel effort at the Opera House in London. The Vicar of St. John's, Keswick, invited his friends to the Lakeside town and thus began in 1875 the series of Conventions for the Deepening of the Spiritual Life which gained for "Keswick" a unique place of leadership in the evangelical world. For a considerable period the majority of its leaders were either evangelists or converts of the 1859 Revival, and quite a number of new speakers had a link with the Revival. It seems to be conclusive that the human engineers of the Keswick Convention were largely the products of the 1859 Revival. Should the critic dismiss the connection of these personalities with both Revival and Convention as accidental, it can be pointed out that, not only was the so-called *Keswick teaching* first announced in Boardman's book in 1860 and propagated by the evangelists of the 1861 phase of the Revival, but Keswick practice of spiritual ecumenicity, as written into the Keswick slogan "All One in Christ Jesus", was borrowed directly from the interdenominational fellowship of Revival days. "Keswick" became the mother of conventions.

Every Revival of religion in the homelands is felt within a decade in the foreign mission-fields, and the records of missionary enterprise and the pages of missionary biography following 1860 are full of clearest evidence of the stimulating effect of the Revival throughout the world. A private letter written by the shrewd and unemotional Church Missionary Society leader, Henry Venn, stated:

"Yet I am so confident that we must either rise on the wave or be overwhelmed by it, that I shall propose on Monday to send a deputation to Ireland to the revival region, to visit the great towns, and to obtain the prayers, sympathy and hearts and hands, if possible, of some of the awakened servants of God. I am anxious thus to connect the Revival with missionary zeal, for the sake of the Revivalists themselves as well as for our cause."

In 1860 the friends of the Revival convened at Liverpool a Conference on Missions. Already, according to Dr. Andrew Somerville, Foreign Mission Secretary of the United Presbyterian Church in Scotland, the Revival was making itself felt on the foreign mission field, and he declared that every letter he had received from foreign missionaries thanked God for increased intercession at home, and expected increased effectiveness abroad. At the Conference the Foreign Secretary of the London Missionary Society, Dr. Arthur Tidman, related the spirit of Revival to the spirit of unity:

"They had heard of those blessed outpourings in America, in Sweden, in Ireland, in Scotland, in various parts of the metropolis, and other places... they had come together knowing that (God) would bless them and be with them from day to day... Let all differences be forgotten: let them not remember that they were Churchmen or Dissenters, Baptists or Wesleyans, Presbyterians or Episcopalians."

The same note was struck by Lord Shaftesbury, who, as chairman of a great public meeting in the Philharmonic Hall during the Conference, said that "this union of all evangelical and orthodox denominations is a great sign of the times," and greeted the conferees as an *Ecumenical Council*. How prophetic were his remarks can be seen in the development of the Ecumenical Missionary Movement. Preceded by trial conferences arranged by Dr. Alexander Duff in New York and London in 1854, the historic Liverpool Conference passed on the task of both to the Mildmay Conference of 1878, followed by the London Conference of 1888, crowned by the Ecumenical Missionary Conference in New York in 1900. Thus the Revival of 1859 helped to lay the foundations of the modern international and interdenominational missionary structure, the International Missionary Council, which Dr. Kenneth S. Latourette dates back "more directly" to the Liverpool Conference of 1860.

The historian, Ernest A. Payne, told of revival in Jamaica:

"The next year, indeed, saw the outbreak of a remarkable spiritual Revival, general throughout the churches of the island. It began in a Moravian church, and spread from the south coast to the central provinces, to Spanish Town and Savanna-la-Mar, from Montego Bay to Ann's Bay, and finally right through the country. Chapels became once more crowded. There was a widespread conviction of sin. Crime diminished. Ethical standards were raised. There was renewed generosity. Old superstitions which had reasserted themselves once more declined in power. As the movement spread, unhealthy excitement and religious hysteria showed themselves in places, but the testimony of almost all observers, of whatever denomination, was that the Revival was a real blessing from God and did permanent good."

The unhealthy excitement and religious hysteria mentioned were understandable in a population of recently emancipated negro slaves. But so great was the improvement in Jamaica that, shortly afterwards, the London Missionary Society decided to withdraw from the field which it had come to regard as an evangelized country.

In 1859, a direct result of the 1858 Awakening in the United States was the beginning of the evangelization of Brazil. Presbyterian missionaries took the lead, followed by Baptists and Methodists, and within three generations the Evangelical constituency in Brazil had exceeded two million. In the 1950s, when the Presbyterian Church of Brazil established a Centenary Commission to celebrate its hundred years of advance by a campaign of revival and evangelism, the total number active in the Evangelical Churches and Sunday-schools of Brazil approximated a million.

Across the South Atlantic, in the year 1860, an extraordinary revival was manifested in the Dutch Reformed Church in Worcester, in the Cape Colony of South Africa. It began with prayer-meetings, and it affected not only the congregations in the towns but showed itself powerfully on remote farms. The pastor of that Dutch Reformed Church in Worcester was one afterwards destined to exercise a powerful ministry in

South Africa and in Britain and America, Andrew Murray. The South African Revival of 1860 affected the Cape, Wellington, Worcester, Montagu, Calvinia, and then spread across the Karoo, stirring congregations in Beaufort West, Murraysburg, Graaff-Reinet, Bloemfontein. More important still, a leader in the 1860 Revival in South Africa, Dominee van der Lingen, proposed to his colleagues in the Dutch Reformed Church that the ten days between Ascension and Pentecost be thereafter devoted to prayer for revival and preaching of evangelism. The records of the past ninety years show clearly that these Pentecost services in the Dutch Reformed Churches have done more to evangelize South Africa than any other agency. Looking back, one is prompted to ask what was the provocation that caused the Revival of 1860 to break forth. The answer is simple. A Conference was held in Worcester in April, 1860, gathering together Dutch and English-speaking missionaries and ministers. Reports were read of the 1858-59 Awakenings in America, Ireland, and Scotland. The result was much prayer for an outpouring of the Holy Spirit.

Before and after the Revival, David Livingstone was turning the bright light of exploration and evangelization upon the Dark Continent of Africa. A lad who (during the Revival) heard him speak, followed in his footsteps, F. S. Arnot, a true pioneer who accomplished a great work as a Brethren missionary and himself led another pioneer, Dan Crawford, into the long grass. The missionary cause in the Congo was immeasurably helped by the arrival of George Grenfell, a great Baptist pioneer and missionary statesman, who testified that his "earliest religious impressions of a serious kind date back to the early 'sixties, when the great wave of awakening that followed the Revival of 1859 was passing over the country". George Grenfell was baptized in Birmingham by the Rev. Samuel Chapman, in 1864. Likewise, the West African pioneer, Mary Slessor of Calabar, was converted in Dundee during the Revival, through the faithful witness of an old woman in a kitchen. Christina Forsyth of Fingoland, a South Africa pioneer, decided the same year, 1859. Mackay of Uganda was converted in 1865.

The Revival was felt in other mission fields. Daily prayer-meetings were begun in Madras, Bombay and Poona and in many parts of India and Burma, besides, in 1859. Dr. Alexander Duff sponsored such meetings in Calcutta, and Anglicans, Presbyterians, Congregationalists and Baptists participated. A great and increasing spirit of prayer prevailed among the Christians in other parts of India. Interest in the subject of religion continued unabated in Delhi in 1860, and a great number of inquirers were seeking baptism. A great Revival broke out in 1860 in Tinnevelly, Madras Presidency, astounding the Anglican missionaries there, for the same controversial "prostrations" were observed as in Ulster and in Scotland, even among heathen. But the Church *Missionary Record* of May 1860 testified of the permanent value of the Tinnevelly Awakening of 1860, specifying 2,500 or more converts. There was a similar ingathering in Chota Nagpore, and such an upsurge of missionary activity that the Lieutenant- Governor of Bengal, a visitor, was amazed. The times of Revival in India in 1859 and 1860 were felt strongly amongst European residents, both civil and military, as, for example, at Sialkot, where there were eleven striking conversions among officers, and many more among the men of the garrison.

The outstanding leader of the Awakening in India was, of course, Dr. Alexander Duff, one of the giants of the Christian Church. In this connection it is apropos to quote Dr. Duff on the 1859 Revival:

"... in face of myriads instantaneously saved under the mighty outpourings of the Spirit of grace, I feel no disposition to enter into argument, discussion or controversy with anyone."

Thus it was that, as India was prepared politically by the changes following the Indian Mutiny of 1857, the missionary enterprises in India were equipped by the outpourings of the Holy Spirit in America, Britain, and amongst missionaries and Indian Christians themselves in India. There were remarkable advances in the evangelization of India following the year 1859, too numerous to chronical here.

To Indonesia went James Chalmers, converted in the Highland Revival of 1859 in Inverary, trained in the Glasgow City Mission -a man whose spiritual life on earth began after he had tried to upset the work of two Ulster evangelists, and ended in a glorious martyrdom in New Guinea.

In 1860 religious revival broke out amongst missionaries in Shanghai. China, at that time, constituted the greatest missionary challenge and opportunity in the world. There were only 115 Protestant missionaries in the whole country, concentrated in coastal cities and river ports. Thanks to the Awakening in America and Britain, the work of established societies revived and new societies were formed in the 1860s. A missionary statesman of the highest order, Timothy Richard, soon came out to China. He had been a convert of the Welsh Revival of 1859, having been baptized on April 10 of that year. James Gilmour of Mongolia was converted in

Glasgow about 1862. In 1866 the missionary forces in China received a 25 per cent increase through the landing of the Lammermuir party of the newly-formed China Inland Mission under the leadership of Hudson Taylor, justly described by Dr. Latourette as one of the greatest missionaries of all time whose programme in China was "unprecedented". The founding of the China Inland Mission was epoch-making in a world-sense as well as in relation to China. The story of the call of James Hudson Taylor is well known, but his relationship to the 1859 Revival and the relationship of the China Inland Mission is unsuspected by all but a few of his admirers. When a missionary of the Chinese Evangelization Society, he received in 1860 a letter from George Pearse:

"You will be glad to know that the Revival has reached London and hundreds are being converted."

And Hudson Taylor, much in need of physical, mental and spiritual recuperation, returned to London that same year.

During his five years' sojourn in London, Hudson Taylor kept no diary, hence his biographer has designated this period "The Hidden Years". The young missionary devoted much of his time to medical studies and translation work. It was impossible that a man of Hudson Taylor's temperament could dwell in London quietly whilst a great Revival was sweeping the metropolis. So Hudson Taylor devoted his spare time, especially his Sundays, to Revivalism in that fruitful training ground, the East End of London. In particular, he laboured in the Twig Folly Mission in Bethnal Green which carried on daily prayer-meetings and preaching services. A noted infidel was converted there, and many converts of the

Revival were baptized as believers. The Revival, then in progress, said Marshall Broomhall, was a revelation in the homeland of God's power to bless, whilst a million a month dying in China without God was its appalling contrast in the mind of the burdened missionary. Whilst visiting George Pearse in Brighton, in the after-glow of the wonderful Brighton Revival, Hudson Taylor faced his life's greatest crisis. On Sunday, June 25, 1865, unable to bear the sight of 1,000 or more Christian people rejoicing in their own security, while multitudes were perishing for lack of knowledge, Hudson Taylor walked the sands and made a great decision.

The prayer-life of British Christians had reached an all-time high. George Müller's example in launching out by faith was being followed elsewhere. The need of China was appreciated by Hudson Taylor as by very few others. So he applied the prayer and faith and action principles of the 1859 Awakening to the need of China, and the China Inland Mission became the extension of that great Revival into the evangelization of the world's most numerous people. Once faith had impelled his steps, where did Hudson Taylor find willing workers for the unprecedented invasion of the kingdom of darkness in China? In 1865 the Laird of Arndilly, Hay Macdowall Grant, used the columns of *The Revival* to invite Christian people to the great Perth Conference, which had been blessing many since the Scottish Revival. Hudson Taylor, a regular reader, proceeded to Perth. On September 6, 1865, after an address by Dr. Andrew Bonar and prayer by R. C. Morgan:

"... the Rev. Mr. Taylor, missionary from China, presented, in a most interesting address, the wants and claims of China, its deeply important character as a field of missionary labour, and the appalling destitution of everything like evangelistic efforts corresponding with her teeming population. He urged on young and devoted Christians to consecrate themselves to this high field of missionary labour..."

So deep an impression was created that *The Revival* gave a couple of columns to a fuller account of the stirring Challenge. The majority of those attending the Perth Conference were Christians awakened in the Revival or actual converts of the Revival. Five of the Lammermuir party which sailed for China the following year were from that part of Scotland, and there is reason to believe that the whole party was made up of converts and workers of the 1859 Awakening. And the Revivalist, George Pearse, wrote:

"The Chinese Evangelization Society... came to an end, but the work itself did not come to an end, for out of the withered roots of this old tree has sprung up a vigorous sapling, which, God grant, may prove to be to the glory of His own blessed name, and the salvation of many precious souls in China."

The example of the China Inland Mission had a profound effect upon the world-wide missionary programme. Interdenominational Faith Missions and other interdenominational societies sprang up until they supplemented the work of the denominational societies all over the earth. The Revival of 1859 set a blessed fashion going. Not all the societies copied the China Inland Mission's constitution wholly, but few there are who owe nothing to it.

CHAPTER TWELVE

CHRISTIAN LEADERS

T HE relationship of the link-personalities of the
Evangelical Revivals is a fascinating story in itself.
A year after the death of John Wesley, Charles Grandison
Finney was born, in 1792. Finney's consuming passion
was that of evangelizing the world by the method of
reviving the church. His work was limited to but a few
states in the United States of America, together with a
couple of visits to Britain. But he became the prophet
of Revival through his famous lectures as well as by
his demonstration of the teaching he advocated. Finney
lived to see the Great Awakening of 1858 onwards, and
participated in it heartily in America and in Britain until
1860.

That year, 1860, the second year of the British
Awakening, was the birth-year of Rodney Smith, who
rose to world prominence as Gipsy Smith. In the darkest
days of reaction the Christian world could not forget the
aggressive evangelism of the nineteenth-century while
Gipsy Smith was a link between the Second Evangelical
Awakening and these world-shaking days of conflict.
Gipsy Smith lived to see the resurgence of evangelism in
the 1940s.

Although prayer-meetings were the greatest vehicle
of blessing in the Awakening of 1858, preaching was by
no means as neglected or discarded as some writers insist.

The authority Beardsley states that in some instances,

"Preaching was employed to promote the revival after it had commenced, but this was exceptional and in most cases there was but little preaching aside from that of the regular Sabbath services. The principal means relied upon were the daily union prayer-meetings."

Dr. Beardsley quotes Charles G. Finney in support of this point of view as follows:

"There was such a general confidence in the prevalence of prayer, that the people very extensively seemed to prefer meetings for prayer to meetings for preaching. The general impression seemed to be 'We have had instruction until we are hardened; it is time for us to pray'."

It is undoubtedly true that reliance upon prayer overshadowed dependence upon preaching, but this conclusion is liable to be misunderstood. Preaching played a secondary part to prayer in the revival, but it played a very good second. Compared with the quantity and quality of the preaching that had preceded the year of the grace, there was truly a great revival of the ministry of preaching. The great focus of interest was the noon prayer-meeting, but the interest there was immediately captured and used by the evening preaching services. The Awakening of 1858 was a revival of preaching, as a careful examination of the foregoing chapters of the narrative shows. The writer is well convinced in his own mind, through reading endless accounts of local situations in the revival, that fully as many people attended the preaching services as the prayer-meetings. There were crowded services every night of the week, and most churches were compelled to hold three and four services on Sunday.

With this fact in mind, let us examine the effect of the Revival upon preaching and preachers.

Dr. Theodore Parker proved to be the Revival's most determined enemy. Another noted liberal, Dr. Horace Bushnell, had his ministry quite transformed by the Revival. Dr. Bushnell's daughter describes the matter in the following words:

"The financial crisis was, as everyone will remember, followed by that great and unexampled religious revival which overspread the country, and moved society to its very foundations. The excitement of it lasted through the whole winter and late into the spring. Ministers, and all those who took an active part in the direction of the great and frequent meetings of the people, were called to make unwonted exertions, and were themselves kept at sustained pitch or strain of feeling that was more exhausting than the work itself. Dr. Bushnell did not spare himself in the services held at his own church, or in the daily union prayer-meetings of the city. Under the pressure of work, and by the aid of sympathy prepared for him in his audiences *he resorted, For the first time, to extempore preaching.* [Italics supplied.] He achieved in this a success unlooked-for, as he had always doubted his ability for offhand speech. Some of these sermons were very remarkable and impressive, and commanded the fixed attention of several intellectual and not hitherto religious men. One day his good friend, Deacon Collins, who had listened to his preaching ever since he had come to Hartford, said as he walked down the aisle, 'Dr. Bushnell must never preach any more written sermons. He may write to print, but not to preach'."

The biographer goes on to explain that by May 1858

Dr. Bushnell was obliged to confess that he was utterly broken down in health through overstrain of preaching and leading prayer-meetings. It was rumoured, not unnaturally, that Horace Bushnell's tremendous evangelism indicated a return to orthodoxy regarding his modified view of the Trinity, but this was not so. Nevertheless, the Awakening caught him up and transformed his ministry for a few short months before his retirement and subsequent decease.

If the Awakening was able thus to transform the ministry of men who were viewed with suspicion by the evangelicals, what would it not have done for orthodox evangelists?

Theodore Ledyard Cuyler gives an introspective picture of the effect of the Revival on his ministry.

"The next stage of my life's work was a seven years' pastorate of Market Street Church in the City of New York. To those seven years of hard and happy labour I look back with joy... During the year 1858 occurred the great revival, when a mighty wind from Heaven filled every house where the people of God were sitting, and the glorious work of that revival kept many of us busy for six months, night and day."

Dr. Cuyler was born in 1822, in the Finger Lakes district of Western New York, the region of the great revivals of the nineteenth century, the habitat of Finney. His widowed mother dedicated him to the service of God. Later he graduated with distinction from Princeton in 1841. The success of a few impromptu remarks of his at a cottage meeting decided him to prepare for the ministry, leading to graduation from Princeton Seminary in 1846.

Theodore Cuyler's first pastorate was in Burlingham, New Jersey, in a small and discouraging church where he was "captain, cook, and cabin-boy" at the same time. Here he started writing religious articles for the press, as an outlet for his energies, a habit which he continued for thirty years until sixty million copies of his articles were published. In the second year of his ministry at Burlingham, a remarkable local revival broke out in his church, doubling his membership and shaping his ministry for life. He became a thorough evangelist. He had further experience in a church in Trenton, but in 1853 he moved to New York City, to the Market Street Dutch Reformed Church, where another local revival attended his ministry. One of his helpers in this church was a quiet-spoken businessman named Jeremiah Lanphier, who, with the help of an elder of the church, M. T. Hewitt, inaugurated a little prayer-meeting in Fulton Street in 1857! Theodore Cuyler threw himself into the programme of the laymen so thoroughly that he soon had become one of the most active workers in the whole movement. He led the first daily prayer-meeting in Burton's Theatre. He led the first daily prayer-meeting in the Ninth Street Church. He opened the first one in lower Broadway. His church received copious showers of blessing in the Awakening. A small church in Brooklyn next called the young divine, and in 1860 his ministry began to stir that city. With an original 140 members, Cuyler built up the work to 1,600 members, then the largest Presbyterian Church in America. In 1866 began a wonderful six months' revival which brought three hundred into the church. Cuyler participated with Moody in the latter's meetings in London in 1873, the beginning of a great awakening in Great Britain. Dr. Cuyler's preaching was devoid of sensationalism. He kept in touch with his flock by means of systematic pastoral calling. The success of his ministry was attributed to his dominant idea that conversion is not an end, but a beginning; an idea of training which he shared with his friend Moody.

Another preacher mightily used in the 1858 Awakening was Henry Ward Beecher. Like Theodore Cuyler, Beecher was already a noted preacher when the revival of religion gave him an unbounded opportunity for his gifts. Besides his own gifts, Henry Ward Beecher was helped by his parentage, being one of the famous children of the famous Lyman Beecher. Henry Ward Beecher became an immediate friend of the 1858 Awakening. On March 20, Mr. Beecher led three thousand people in the prayer service in Burton's Theatre in New York, and from that time onwards, he revelled in the work. Newspapers were impressed by Beecher's support of the movement, and were glad to quote any words he uttered about the Revival. It is interesting to note that on March 25, 1858, the New York Young Men's Christian Union postponed a series of lectures by Henry Ward Beecher and Horace Greeley in order to have a debate on revivals in general and the current revival in particular, a debate that was highly favourable, according to the *New York Herald* of that date. It is quite likely that Henry Ward Beecher was too busily preoccupied in the Revival to come and lecture. The occurrence of his name in report after report in the press substantiates this view.

New York being the centre of the Awakening, Henry Ward Beecher was the leading spokesman for the movement in New York and throughout the United States as well. He was a great acquisition. His powers as a preacher were never put to better use, and seldom received such sympathetic response. Says a biographer:

"It was in the pulpit that Beecher was seen at his best. His mastery of the English tongue, his dramatic power, his instinctive art of impersonation, which had become a second nature, his vivid imagination, his breadth of intellectual view, the catholicity of his sympathies, his passionate enthusiasm, which made for the moment his immediate theme seem to be the one theme of transcendent importance, his quaint humour alternating with genuine pathos, and above all his simple and singularly unaffected devotional nature, made him a preacher without a peer in his own time and country."

Very different from Beecher in many respects, but with a fame which outshone him in succeeding generations, was Charles Grandison Finney, who was greatly used of God during the 1858 Revival. The 1858 movement taught Finney little about revivals, for he himself was the storm centre of revivals for a generation previously. Indeed, the Awakening of 1858 seemed to be a justification of all that Finney had taught in his famous *Lectures on Revivals of Religion*. Charles Grandison Finney's preaching was of a type to suit the age in which he lived. At that time, such strong Calvinistic doctrines as God's sovereignty, Man's inability, Election, Reprobation, and the like had been taught to extremes, bringing about a paralysis among the people in the matters of responsibility and decision. Finney, on the other hand, taught that men were responsible for their sins, and that they were sinners because they chose to be, and that they ought to repent as the Lord had so commanded them. It was also noteworthy that Finney always preached for immediate decision, trying to make the individual choose then and there to do something. He was the most direct preacher of his day. The 1858 Awakening found Finney in Boston, and his soul rejoiced over what he saw in that metropolis. Where before the revival had centred in his own ministry, now every church was experiencing blessing. Finney worked hard until he left for England that same year.

Besides those outstanding men, there were hundreds of others who were given their life's greatest opportunity in the Awakening. The records of the day show that most pastors were busy from morning to night preaching and presiding at meetings. As to what they preached it is clear from the fragments of sermons and addresses appearing in newspapers that the doctrine was evangelical and the method evangelistic. No other type of preaching could have found a place in the revival.

An American observer, commenting upon the spread of the Revival in America and Britain, noted the influence of the prayer-meeting movement in both countries, then pointed out:

"As the work spread into Great Britain, new features appeared. Gifts which seemed to exist (in America) in a sort of general diffusion among Christian people, were there vouchsafed in greater intensity to individuals. Men appeared as chosen instruments of conveying God's truth to the aroused and interested masses. Lay and clerical evangelists, conspicuous for zeal, enjoying the special favour of God, and devoting themselves exclusively to the work, contributed to extend and deepen its sphere and to multiply its fruits. No such characters appeared in this country as Richard Weaver, Reginald Radcliffe, Brownlow North, and E. P. Hammond, whereas in Great Britain the spirit of Revival culminated in these persons.

"Some in America may congratulate us as, so far, better off than the British people, but we differ from them. Had a class of men, preeminently endowed for the work, been in like manner raised up among us; had some American

Radcliffe or Weaver been divinely commissoned to speak to the poor and outcast of our cities at that time, the result must have been far in advance of what we actually beheld. The Infinite Spirit in his sovereign appointment did not see fit to bestow upon us this crowning gift—a personal embodiment and representative of the work—a Leader whom all might recognize, and who might have marshalled the Christian hosts to far greater victories even than those which they did achieve."

When those words were written, the armies of the Union and the Confederacy were locked in a Titanic struggle. An American leader, not until afterwards generally recognized, was already busy in a steady ministry to soldiers and civilians in camps and cities: and the Infinite Spirit was soon to give Dwight L. Moody an opportunity of moving mightily two great countries.

The emergence of leaders in Great Britain was a distinct feature of the British Awakening of the 1860s. In Ulster the movement was more like that of the American Revival of 1858, a spontaneous, leaderless turning to God. In Wales, excepting the work of David Morgan, it was the same. In Scotland a number of prepared evangelists participated in the general Awakening there, and then moved south for a greater work to be done in England. And in England, as in Southern Ireland, the emerging evangelists—both workers and converts of the first period of Revival—accomplished the main mission of the Awakening.

Nearly all the much-used evangelists in England were witnesses of the intense Revivals in Ulster, Scotland, and Wales. The Palmers had seen the Spirit at work in Canada and America, and the Booths doubtless witnessed the startling Revival across the Tyne from Gateshead.

Most of them, therefore, served their apprenticeship in a spontaneous type of Revival, and carried the fire to less combustible areas, where the fuel had to be first gathered and dried of the damp of indifference. The evangelists of the British Awakening were of various denominational loyalties within the evangelical school of thought. The records of the Revival reveal no clashes between them, and they seemed to work like members of a very agreeable family. There was a division of labour according to the evangelist's background. The converted chimney-sweep did not attempt drawing-room meetings for the élite of society, and the converted aristocrat did not form Hallelujah Bands of cock-fighters, bear wrestlers, prizefighters, and jail-birds. But they helped one another, and introduced one another to suitable opportunities.

Among American contributions to the rank of British evangelists in the Revival was a devout Methodist, James Caughey, through whom William Booth was brought to decision in his youth. The Wesleyan leaders in control of the societies excluded the American from their pulpits, but he continued his ministry in the pulpits remaining open in several Methodist bodies. James Caughey belonged to an earlier generation of evangelists, and had been in Britain several times before.

Edward Payson Hammond was born in the Connecticut Valley in 1831. He was converted seventeen years later, and laboured in the American Revival of 1858. Visiting Scotland for purposes of self-improvement, young Hammond was asked to preach in Musselburgh in 1860, during the Scottish Awakening. Having left his great-coat in the vestry, he proceeded there, but found it bolted. A very little girl opened it, and explained that "a wheen o'us lassies" were there. Hammond overheard a tiny tot offer such a beautiful prayer that tears came to his eyes. His ideas were soon revolutionized. He became the children's evangelist, and foster-father of the Children's Special Service Mission. Hammond accomplished great work in his Revival services in the Vale of Dumfries and in Glasgow and elsewhere in Britain and America. But his greatest work was as a winner of children to Christ. In the late 1860's Spurgeon filled the Metropolitan Tabernacle with 8,000 children to hear Hammond preach. Seventeen years later Payson Hammond returned to find that some of the child converts were Spurgeon's workers.

Apart from a steady stream of reports of successful campaigns, there is very little material available in Britain on the life-work of Walter C. Palmer and his wife Phoebe. Methodists, stirred by the original outbreak of Revival in Hamilton, Ontario, they crossed to Britain and continued in evangelism for five years. Like Caughey, and his convert Booth, they were excluded from many Methodist pulpits. Dr. Palmer appeared to be a layman, a doctor of medicine. His work as a physician and surgeon of souls has a large place in the foregoing narrative. His wife's example inspired Catherine Booth to preach, and so led to the Salvation Army bonnet-ministry.

Foremost among the British leaders of the 1859 Revival was Henry Grattan Guinness, a preacher of great power for half a century. He was born in 1835, in Kingstown, near Dublin. In his first twenty years he indulged his adventurous desires in globetrotting, then he came under deep conviction of sin and was converted. Grattan Guinness was the most popular evangelist in Ulster during the 1859 Revival, and, on one occasion, he addressed 20,000 people from the top of a cab. Fifty years afterwards the memory was still vivid with him:

"... the predominating feature was the conversion of people of all ranks and positions, in ways sudden, startling, amazing... Before that time, I had seen tens, or scores, brought to Christ under Gospel preaching; but this new movement of 1859 was something quite different... Ministers were occupied until midnight, or even till two or three o'clock in the morning, conversing with crowds of inquirers who were crying: 'What shall I do to be saved?'"

It was at the house of Grattan Guinness that Tom Barnardo met Hudson Taylor. After the crest of the Revival years had passed, H. Grattan Guinness began to take an ever-deepening interest in foreign missions. His greatest contribution to the Christian Church was surely in winning multiplied thousands of converts in the days of the Revival, and in training 1,330 men and women for missionary service under thirty denominations in forty missionary societies. Dr. Tom Barnardo, on holiday in Venice, said: "I can never tell what Guinness has done for me; it is through him that I am what I am."

Among other outstanding men of God who became harvesters of the Years of Grace were several gentlemen-evangelists, Brownlow North, Grant of Arndilly, Reginald Radcliffe, and Gordon Forlong, all of whom were much-used evangelists when the Revival began, but whose ministry developed phenomenally in Revival opportunities.

Similar to the group of gentlemen-evangelists was a group of working-men evangelists, Richard Weaver, Duncan Matheson, John Hambledon, James Turner, and William Carter, each of whom was busy in evangelism before the 1859 Awakening but developed amazingly during the Revival movement.

Among the Pastoral Evangelists of the Awakening were William Pennefather, William Haslam, Samuel Garratt, John Venn, C. H. Spurgeon, Baptist Noel, Henry Varley, Newman Hall, Denham Smith, Andrew Bonar, Horatio Bonar, David Morgan, and many others in both State Church and Nonconformity.

Several of the Church of England's most spiritual and successful Bishops were "impressed" in the Revival of 1859. Perhaps the most outstanding were F. J. Chavasse of Oxford and Handley C. G. Moule of Cambridge, whose spiritual unfolding in the Awakening has been noted. The former became Bishop of Liverpool, following in the footsteps of the evangelical, Bishop Ryle, himself active in the Revival in Suffolk. The latter became Bishop of Durham, in the succession to the evangelical, Bishop Baring, another active evangelist of the time.

The conversion in Revival times of James Chalmers of New Guinea, Christina Forsyth of Fingoland, James Gilmour of Mongolia, George Grenfell of the Congo, Timothy Richard of China, and Mary Slessor of Calabar, has already been noted in the narrative. Research in missionary biography and obituary notices would doubtless reveal many other converts of the Awakening who made their contribution to foreign missions.

The Methodist Conference of 1903 described Hugh Price Hughes as one of the most conspicuous and successful ministers ever ordained within its fellowship, and said that no Methodist minister was ever more widely lamented. Hugh Price Hughes (partly of Jewish stock) was converted in the Welsh Revival in 1860, at the age of thirteen. He was an ardent evangelist, an advocate of temperance, an agitator for social purity.

Dr. Hugh Black of Edinburgh described John McNeill,

Scottish preacher of Ulster parentage, as the greatest living preacher in his day, rather than Joseph Parker, Alexander MacLaren or Alexander Whyte. John McNeill was converted in the after-glow of the Scottish Revival, and gave his own testimony of the impression made upon his young mind in 1869 when the tide of Revival was still running.

Dr. F. B. Meyer was baptized upon confession of faith in New Park Road Chapel, near Denmark Hill, on June 2, 1864. Meyer had been brought up in a Christian home in London, and had grown in grace in childhood; but it was during the Revival in the metropolis that he heard the call to the ministry and entered upon a truly fragrant life of service. From his first sponsoring of Moody to his founding of the National Young Life Campaign with the Brothers Wood in the present century he was an ardent evangelist.

The striking conversion of Harry Moorhouse in Manchester, and his subsequent ministry in Britain and America, have been described already, with particular emphasis upon his profound influence on the ministry of Dwight L. Moody.

William Robertson Nicol, the noted editor of the *British Weekly* and as great a figure in British life generally as in Nonconformist circles, was an indirect product of the Scottish Revival of 1859. He always declared that this Revival made a deep impression on his young mind, for he was only nine years of age when he came under the influence of the great gatherings organized by Elizabeth, Duchess of Gordon, one of the Revival's greatest supporters.

Professor James Orr, the Scottish theologian, was born in a Christian family but fell under the influence of sceptics in his teens, the noted infidel Joseph Barker particularly disturbing him. During the Scottish Revival he was converted, and shortly afterwards entered Glasgow University.

Actually impressed by the Awakening was the Rev. Alexander Whyte, of whom, in his *Preachers I Have Heard*, Alexander Gammie states:

"There has been no preacher in living memory of greater personality, preaching power, and abiding influence than Dr. Alexander Whyte, of St. George's Edinburgh... He was the last of the Puritans."

Alexander Whyte was revived in the Scottish Awakening of 1859 onwards. He was a student at the time of the outbreak in Aberdeen, and was caught up in the work much as Hay Aitken. Fifty years later Dr. Whyte's memories of the Revival were so vivid that he penned his *Reminiscences of the Revival of '59*. Its pages show how deeply his life was influenced by the outpouring of the Holy Spirit in his youth. As an old man, he averred:

"... a Revival quickens dead men, touches men's imaginations and sets loose their hearts... There is a Divine mystery about Revivals. God's sovereignty is in them."

The great Scottish preacher looked forward as well as back, saying:

"I may not live to see it. But the day will come when there will be a great Revival over the whole earth."

CHAPTER THIRTEEN

REVIVAL THEOLOGY

THE 1858-59 Awakening was an Evangelical Revival in the truest sense of the word. It was supported by Evangelical Christians of all varieties, and it strengthened Evangelical Christians of all varieties. It was not supported by Roman Catholics, Anglo-Catholics or Unitarians, and it seemed to contribute nothing to Roman Catholicism, Anglo-Catholicism and Unitarianism.

The Awakening affected impartially the two great divisions of Evangelicalism, the Calvinist and the Arminian. The Revival was seen at its greatest intensity among the traditionally Calvinistic denominations of Ulster, Scotland and Wales: and yet it affected as powerfully the ultra-Methodist groups in Cornwall and produced the Salvation Army, a convinced Arminian fellowship. In America there was no distinction at all.

In the Awakening the two systems of interpretation were not reconciled. Rather they were blended. There was little friction between Calvinists and Arminians anywhere. One of the few instances uncovered by this research will suffice to show how mild the friction was: *The Watchman*, a London Methodist periodical, complained that, in the united prayer-meetings in Bath, the Baptists, Congregationalists and Churchmen seemed to avoid instinctively such controversial questions as Baptism and Church Government, yet they kept on praying the most

Calvinistic prayers! *The Watchman* might have added that, although the Revivalists prayed like Calvinists, they worked like Arminians for the salvation of souls. Though the Calvinist-Arminian controversy had been extremely bitter following the first Evangelical Revival, there was the happiest harmony during the Second Evangelical Awakening.

There were no serious charges made by Evangelical Theologians on doctrinal grounds against the teaching of the Revivalists. Objections from the traditionalist and liberalist sections of Christendom were expected and experienced: but, among Evangelicals, while some cloistered thinkers shook their heads over the phenomena and excitement of the Revival, few were able to raise a doctrinal issue.

In England, *The Record* published some strictures upon the methods of the Revivalists (Denham Smith in particular). Its correspondent in Geneva complained that the awakened sinner had been told that he could only obtain peace through faith in the atoning blood of Christ, and was left to seek in his own natural strength for the attainment of this primary of all Christian graces, instead of being directed to apply for the help of the Holy Spirit. The Rev. Samuel Garratt, a London clergyman, replied that the Scriptural method was to tell the awakened sinners to repent and be baptized and they would receive the gift of the Holy Ghost. The Geneva Correspondent complained of the welcome immediately given the new convert, suggesting that the convert had no hope of the glorious promises of the Gospel until he had demonstrated a complete change of heart. Samuel Garratt replied that the objector was looking for the fruits before the tree, and reversing the order of Scripture.

There was nothing new in the theology of the nineteenth-century Revival. All of its teachings were derived from the New Testament, and many of its strong points were doctrines recovered in the Reformation and re-emphasized in the Evangelical Revival of the eighteenth century. The Revivalists as a whole shared the doctrinal views of the Evangelical Alliance on seven points:

"I. The Divine Inspiration, Authority and Sufficiency of the Holy Scriptures, and the right and duty of Private Judgment in the interpretation thereof.

"II. The Unity of the Godhead, and the Trinity of Persons therein.

"III. The utter Depravity of Human Nature, in consequence of the Fall.

"IV. The Incarnation of the Son of God, His work of Atonement for sinners of mankind, and His Mediatorial Intercession and Reign.

"V. The Justification of the sinner by Faith alone.

"VI. The work of the Holy Spirit in the Conversion and Sanctification of the sinner.

"VII. The Resurrection of the Body, the Judgment of the world by the Lord Jesus Christ, the Eternal Blessedness of the Righteous, and the Eternal Punishment of the Wicked."

The Evangelical Alliance had adopted a final statement of faith—that of the Divine Institution of the Christian Ministry and the Obligation and Perpetuity of the Ordinances of Baptism and the Lord's Supper. The records of the Revival reveal no departure from the points listed above, but they do indicate the participation of preachers and teachers, such as Brethren and Quaker, whose view of Christian ministry and the Ordinances was different to that of most denominations.

In addition to the body of doctrine shared by the supporters of the Revival, the Evangelical Alliance view of Christian Unity was so widely adopted that it led to a practice of fraternal fellowship having the force of a major doctrine. This view of Christian Unity was held by the early Brethren as a doctrine of the Church, but the rise of the Darby interpretation of it rent the Brethren into a score of fragments, with two major divisions— the Exclusive Brethren who followed Darby, and the Open Brethren who followed Müller in his insistence upon the freedom of fellowship with all those whom the Lord Jesus had received. The early Brethren view of Christian Unity gradually permeated the thinking of the Evangelical denominations via the Evangelical Alliance and the Evangelical Awakening of 1858-59.

As already shown, the Keswick Convention Movement, with its doctrine of Scriptural Holiness by Faith, grew out of the 1858-59 Revival, though, of course, the doctrine was by no means adopted by all Evangelicals, let alone the followers of the Revival. The Salvation Army, for example, adopted a much more Wesleyan view of Holiness. In 1947, however, the Keswick Convention welcomed its first Salvationist speaker, Major Allister Smith, whose ministry represented both points of view.

The expansion of the Christian Church in the years following the Awakening strengthened some Evangelicals in their view of world evangelization, which supposed the gradual betterment of the world until the Kingdom of God became dominant everywhere, and Christ reigned invisibly in the hearts of men. The doctrine held strongly by the Brethren ran counter to his view. They, not alone, held a catastrophic view of eschatology, believing in world evangelization for the purpose of gathering out a redeemed Church, in the worsening of world conditions (save in science and travel and education) followed by the return of Christ in a personal and visible manner. The former view. of world evangelization is held strongly today by Liberal Evangelicals, whilst Conservative Evangelicals have been more and more influenced by the Brethren interpretations of Scripture—not necessarily following Brethren "experts" into all their prophetical theories. It seems fair to say that the majority of the present-day adherents of the 1858-59 Revival tradition have adopted the catastrophic view of eschatology. The influence of the Revival in this matter has been indirect, for it emphasized the "conservative" view of the Scriptures which led to the adoption of a "conservative" eschatology.

All things considered, the nineteenth-century Awakening represented no great discovery or rediscovery of doctrine. Its theology was largely that of the New Testament stated in the language of the Reformers and the Revivalists of an earlier century. The great contribution of the Awakening was its application of these doctrines in the evangelization of the great mass of unchurched at home and the heathen abroad.

CHAPTER FOURTEEN

REVIVAL HYMNOLOGY

O F NECESSITY there is a time lag in the effect of any Evangelical Awakening upon the hymn-singing of the people moved by it. Until newly-inspired writers compose verses and tunes, the singing congregations must use old hymns. Hence, the hymns of the Evangelical Revival of the eighteenth century enjoyed a fresh popularity during the Awakening of the nineteenth century, the spiritual songs of the Wesleys and Watts being the prime favourites. The records of the nineteenth-century Revival are full of reports of the singing of old hymns with new meaning. As the experiences of the former Revival were relived, the overflowing songs of salvation and sanctification were judged the best expression of the praise which welled in the hearts of redeemed people.

A demand for hymn-books arose. In the early sixties, according to Julian's *Dictionary of Hymnology*, a large mass of Churchmen were prepared for hymns of a moderate, definite and popular character, and so, in 1861, *Hymns Ancient and Modern*, now the standard book of the Church of England, was published. This book was used in chapels as well as Established churches, though the Nonconformists generally preferred to use their own books.

A prime favourite was

> "There is a fountain filled with blood,
> Drawn from Emmanuel's veins;

> And singers plunged beneath that flood
> Lose all their guilty stains."

Similarly, Charles Wesley's words

> "My chains fell off,
> My heart was free;
> I rose, went forth,
> And followed Thee,"

were full of deep meaning to the thousands of converts being reached by the converted cock-fighters, gamblers, drunkards and bear-wrestlers in the Midlands.

The earliest favourite of the Ulster Awakening was a piece of doggerel verse composed by a young Scotsman. Very few Ulster Christians know it today, but one recalls having heard veterans of Victorian times singing it. Neither the poetry nor the music are in the least "distinguished", but it is recognizable as a hymn of experience, and it was broadcast by the tens of thousands in America and Britain.

> "Where'er we meet, you always say,
>   What's the news? what's the news?
> Pray, what's the order of the day?
>   What's the news? what's the news?
> Oh! I have got good news to tell;
> My Saviour hath done all things well,
> And triumphed over death and hell,
>   That's the news! that's the news!
>
> The Lamb was slain on Calvary,
>   That's the news! that's the news!
> To set a world of sinners free,
>   That's the news! that's the news!
> 'Twas there His precious blood was shed,
> 'Twas there he bowed His sacred head;
> But now he's risen from the dead,

That's the news! that's the news!

To heav'n above the Conqueror's gone,
   That's the news! that's the news!
He's passed triumphant to His throne,
   That's the news! that's the news!
And on that throne He will remain
Until as Judge He comes again,
Attended by a dazzling train,
   That's the news! that's the news!

His work's reviving all around—
   That's the news! that's the news!
And many have redemption found—
   That's the news! that's the news!
And since their souls have caught the flame,
They shout Hosanna to His name;
And all around they spread His fame—
   That's the news! that's the news!

The Lord has pardoned all my sin—
   That's the news! that's the news!
I feel the witness now within—
   That's the news! that's the news!
And since He took my sins away
And taught me how to watch and pray,
I'm happy now from day to day—
   That's the news! that's the news!

And Christ the Lord can save you, too—
   That's the news! that's the news!
Your sinful heart He can renew—
   That's the news! that's the news!
This moment, if for sins you grieve,
This moment if you do believe,
A full acquittal you'll receive—

That's the news! that's the news!

And now, if anyone should say,
    What's the news? what's the news?
Oh, tell them you've begun to pray—
    That's the news! that's the news!
That you have joined the conquering band,
And now with joy at God's command,
You're marching to the better land—
    That's the news! that's the news!"

A contemporary writer, noting the upsurge of evangelistic singing in the American Awakening, commented:

"One of the incidental effects of the large religious meetings held every day in various quarters of the city has been to increase to an unusual degree the demand for hymn-books to be used in the devotional exercises of the meetings, and tracts to be distributed by persons who take an active part in promoting the movement. The hymn-book in general use in the prayer-meetings is a little collection, common in Sunday-schools, that can be bought for a few cents, and thus scattered in great numbers through the pews at a trifling cost.

"The whole perplexity how to have good church music, is solved by hearing one hymn sung in the Chambers Street or John Street prayer-meeting. The observer will be struck with the unity of time and movement throughout that vast and unschooled chorus. Not a voice can be heard to 'drag', on the most familiar air that has been drawled out in sleepy meetings for a hundred years. Every note is awake, prompt and eager in its rhythmical place. The physical imperfections of voice and ear, which, in a choir of from twenty to fifty persons, might be almost intolerable, are as little thought of as the hoarser notes in the thunder of the ocean or the roar of the forest."

The great meeting in Jayne's Hall in Philadelphia gave birth to a hymn that found its way into the hymnology of the Christian church of all ages. In that vast throng of praying people was a young man named George Duffield, who was stirred profoundly by what he saw and heard. The result was the hymn:

> "Stand up, stand up for Jesus,
>   Ye soldiers of the cross,
> Lift high His royal banner,
>   It must not suffer loss;
> From victory unto victory
>   His army He shall lead,
> Till every foe is vanquished,
>   And Christ is Lord indeed.
>
> Stand up, stand up for Jesus,
>   The trumpet call obey,
> Forth to the mighty conflict,
>   In this His glorious day;
> Ye that are men now serve Him
>   Against unnumbered foes;
> Let courage rise with danger,
>   And strength to strength oppose.
>
> Stand up, stand up for Jesus,
>   Stand in His strength alone;
> The arm of flesh will fail you,
>   Ye dare not trust your own;
> Put on the gospel armour,
>   Each piece put on with prayer;
> Where duty calls, or danger,
>   Be never wanting there.

> Stand up, stand up for Jesus,
> The strife will not be long;
> This day the noise of battle,
> The next the victor's song;
> To him that overcometh
> A crown of life shall be,
> He with the King of Glory
> Shall reign eternally."

When the news of the remarkable Awakenings in America and Ireland reached London, Mrs. Elizabeth Codner composed her heart-prayer that still strikes deep cords in the human heart:

> "Lord, I hear of show'rs of blessing
> Thou art scatt'ring full and free,—
> Show'rs, the thirsty land refreshing;
> Let Thy blessing fall on me—even me.
>
> Pass me not, O gracious Father!
> Sinful though my heart may be;
> Thou might'st leave me, but the rather
> Let Thy mercy fall on me—even me.
>
> Pass me not, O tender Saviour!
> Let me love and cling to Thee;
> I am longing for Thy favour;
> Whilst Thou'rt calling, O call me—even me.
>
> Pass me not, O mighty Spirit!
> Thou canst make the blind to see;
> Witnesser of Jesus' merit,
> Speak the word of power to me—even me.
>
> Love of God, so pure and changeless;
> Blood of Christ, so rich and free;
> Grace of God, so strong and boundless;

Magnify them all in me—even me."

The Revival, with its finger-tips on the public pulse, began to publish a hymn each week. One hymn, written in 1836, became popular in the English-speaking world through the nineteenth-century Awakening, for the 1859 Revival in Britain introduced Charlotte Elliott's "*Just as I am*" to the great congregations of the movement.

> "Just as I am, without one plea,
>   But that Thy blood was shed for me,
> And that Thou bidst me come to Thee,
>   O Lamb of God, I come.
>
> Just as I am, and waiting not
>   To rid my soul of one dark blot,
> To Thee, whose blood can cleanse each spot,
>   O Lamb of God, I come.
>
> Just as I am, Thou wilt receive,
>   Wilt welcome, pardon, cleanse, relieve;
> Because Thy promise I believe,
>   O Lamb of God, I come.
>
> Just as I am, Thy love unknown
>   Has broken every barrier down;
> Now to be Thine, yea, Thine alone,
>   O Lamb of God, I come."

This remains the greatest of all hymns of evangelistic invitation and multitudes of decisions have been made through it in every generation since.

The Revival popularized another already published hymn which was proving extremely effective.

> "O happy Day that fixed my choice
>   On Thee, my Saviour and my God!

Well may this glowing heart rejoice
And tell its raptures all abroad."

By and by new hymns appeared. William Pennefather composed a beautiful hymn of invocation in 1860:

"Jesu stand among us
In Thy risen power:
Let this time of worship
Be a hallowed hour."

Elizabeth Cecilia Clephane (died 1869) composed several poems during the period of the Revival, which were afterwards set to music. One such was:

"Beneath the Cross of Jesus
I fain would take my stand."

Another was set to music by the great American singer, Ira Sankey,

"There were ninety and nine that safely lay
In the shelter of the fold."

But the greatest effect of the Revival upon British hymnology was its introduction of the hymns of the American Gospel-singers, which burst upon Britain like a flood during the Moody and Sankey campaigns in the 1870s.

Philip P. Bliss was deeply moved by the preaching of the young convert of the Manchester Revival, Harry Moorhouse, on John iii. 16. He wrote a hymn with the sentiments of the sermon:

"Whosoever heareth, shout, shout the sound,
Send the blessed tidings all the world around,
Spread the joyful news wherever man is found:
'Whosoever will may come.'"

In quick succession, Philip P. Bliss composed *"Almost Persuaded"*, *"Ho, My Comrades"*, *"Pull for the Shore, Sailor!"*, *"More Holiness Give Me"*, *"Standing to a Purpose True"*, *"Let the Lower Lights Be Burning"*, *"Free From the Law"*, *"The Whole World was Lost in the Darkness of Sin"*, *"Man of Sorrows"*, *"Sing Them Over Again to Me"*, and others of the kind, until his death in a railway disaster in Ohio.

The new American Gospel hymns were introduced by Moody and Sankey. They had little of the elegance of the composition of Charles Wesley, and they used popular style of music with repetitious refrains. But they were eagerly taken up by the masses in Great Britain, and they remain the prime favourites for evangelistic meetings to this day. The British publishers[1] have sold more than 90,000,000 Sankey hymn-books in less than eighty years. They have sold many millions more of Alexander's hymn-book. Other publishers have popularized the same hymns in other compilations.

With these examples in mind, it can be said that the 1859 Revival made a profound impression upon British hymnology, and revolutionized the singing in evangelistic meetings.

[1]Marshall, Morgan Scott, London.

CHAPTER FIFTEEN

NINETEENTH-CENTURY AWAKENING

THE FOREGOING pages have endeavoured to survey the course of the great religious Revival of the nineteenth century throughout the United States and Britain and to study its effects upon the religious and social life.

In final summary, certain facts need to be high-lighted. The most important is that the movement cannot be considered apart from the regular current of Christian life, or restricted to the passage of the seven years considered in detail here.

Only when the bulk of the foregoing material had been assembled was it possible to gain a comprehensive view of the Awakening and its relationship to the movements of the fifty years following. It has been concluded that the fifty years following 1858 constituted a distinct and definite period of the expansion of the Christian Church, in fact, a nineteenth-century evangelical Awakening comparable to its noted predecessor of the eighteenth century.

The first phase began in the Revival of religion which followed an outpouring of the Holy Spirit, first clearly manifested in the remarkable movement of prayer with its attendant conviction of sin. In the general sense, leaderless, this Revival became the means of winning hundreds of thousands to the Christian way of life. Its peak passed, but the Christian communities were by then operating upon a higher level of spiritual effectiveness.

The second phase took its rise in the development of evangelism. Dwight L. Moody, whose Christian service actually began during the first phase of the Awakening, after 1873 became a force in Britain as well as America. Moody extended the scope and the methods of the same Awakening, for he introduced little that was new. His united prayer-meetings, co-operative evangelism, zeal for home and foreign missions, promotion of lay ministry, development of leadership, dependence on the Scriptures—all these were already in evidence in the movement of 1858 which affected young Moody's life in Chicago. Moody was, without question, the greatest single product of the Revival. But he was not alone in his heyday of usefulness from 1873 to 1899. Those years were outstanding in the history of the expansion of English-speaking Christianity.

The third phase of the Awakening began shortly after the turn of the century. Like the first, it manifested another outpouring of the Spirit of prayer with its accompanying conviction of sin. Its effects were seen in sharpest focus in the Welsh Revival of 1905 under hortatory preaching of Evan Roberts. It had also an evangelistic phase in the world-wide ministry of Reuben Torrey and Wilbur Chapman, who, with their team-mate Charles M. Alexander, led great evangelistic campaigns in Australasia, Britain and North America. The third phase closed before the outbreak of the First World War.

The relating of these three movements as a period of fifty years of expansion, a Second Evangelical Awakening or Nineteenth Century Revival, is a new thesis, so far as one can gather.[1] Why this new view had not been stated before is a mystery. Perhaps it required the passing of time to give the proper perspective. Church historians unite in recognizing gratefully the Moody period of evangelism in Britain and America. The period should be advanced fifteen years to date from the year 1858, when Moody served his apprenticeship (so to speak) in Chicago during the world-wide Revival of religion; and it should be extended fifteen years after his death to include the work of Moody-type evangelism and Revival terminated by the First World War.

*   *   *   *   *

A further conclusion is reached that the Second Evangelical Awakening, *even when considered only in its first phase*, was of the same magnitude as well as the same order as the eighteenth-century Evangelical Revival. To make this clear, the following condensed summary is given:

Geographically, the 1858-9 Evangelical Awakening affected Christian communities in every part of Canada, the United States, England, Scotland, Wales, and Ulster, as the reports collated in this narrative indicate. In this respect, the movement was every bit as effective as the earlier Evangelical Awakening which stirred the three kingdoms and the thirteen colonies.

---

[1] The only confirmation received so far came from the bedside of an aged historian, now deceased, Mrs. Howard Taylor, nee Geraldine Guinness, daughter of Dr. H. Grattan Guinness of Revivalist fame, and daughter-in-law of Dr. J. Hudson Taylor. Mrs. Taylor, deeply interested to learn of the present project, said: "Christian people do not seem to realize the importance of that wonderful Revival of 1859. It lasted fifty years... *fifty years*!"

Numerically, the 1858-9 Awakening added approximately 2,000,000 converts to the various churches, and the available testimony suggests that the quality of the conversions was excellent and abiding. The revivalist preaching of the Wesleys, Whitefield and their contemporaries had deeply moved a vast mass of human beings, as stated by Dr. Trevelyan. Without doubt the Second Evangelical Awakening moved a greater mass of human beings, for the population had doubled in the intervening period. In its setting, the Wesleyan Revival was incomparably effective; but the fact remains that no historian would claim 2,000,000 converts in five years for the redoubtable Wesley and his companions. His great work was spread over a life-time of untiring service, and there were 76,000 members connected with his British Methodist societies when he died, though his spiritual inheritors must have been several times that number, considering Evangelicals of all affiliations.

Denominationally, every evangelical church fellowship gained from the 1858-9 Revival. Their gains were proportionate to their evangelical-evangelistic strength, and inversely proportionate to the strength of anti-evangelical traditions among them. Only one new denomination grew out of the Awakening, the Salvation Army, not a cleavage but rather the consolidation of a remarkably effective Home Mission effort which still enjoys the support of other denominational Christians.

Evangelistically, the 1858-9 Awakening revived the older agencies raised up by the Evangelical Revival of the previous century. It also created new organizations of a permanent character, and increased the efforts of all Christians to fulfil the Great Commission to preach the Gospel to every creature, at home and abroad.

Socially, the 1858-9 Awakening gave birth to a litter of active religious and philanthropic societies, which accomplished much in human uplift, the welfare of children, the reclamation of prostituted women, of alcoholics, of criminals, and the development of social virtues.

Individually, the 1858-9 Awakening presented the Church and people with a crop of sturdy husbandmen in every field of life, contributing to the general store the priceless fruits of sanctified personality.

Certain effects of the Awakening are not immediately apparent—the relation of the conversion of hundreds of thousands, who developed an insatiable desire for education, to the passing of the British 1870 Education Act: or the evangelical conversion of Keir Hardie under Moody's ministry and the introduction of that evangelical spirit into the Labour Movement in contrast to the atheism of Continental socialism.

*   *   *   *   *

In his epic *English Social History*, Dr. G. M. Trevelyan points out that the Reformation effected under the Tudors was at once a political, a religious and a social event.

The great Evangelical Revival of the eighteenth century was also effective in all three spheres of life: it prepared America for a theistic republic and it saved Britain from a bloody Revolution; it produced the Evangelical order within the Church of England, and Methodism, and revived Nonconformity without; and it changed the social order by stages, spectacularly in the abolition of slavery. But the Evangelical Revival of the eighteenth century, unlike the Reformation, owed little or nothing to the play and counterplay of political forces. Instead of producing a revolutionary development, it made possible an evolutionary development, achieving as much liberty, equality and fraternity in the long run by less harmful means.

Compared with the eighteenth-century Revival, the Evangelical Awakening of the nineteenth century had even fewer political sources and less political effect, though it is noteworthy that, within its scope of fifty years, the expansion of the English-speaking world was effected— the preservation of the Union of American States being achieved in the 1860s, followed by the Confederation of Canada, and the maturing of Australia, and New Zealand, and the Union of South Africa. As the Evangelical Revival of the eighteenth-century was chiefly religious and social in its manifestations, so also was the Evangelical Awakening of the nineteenth century. Perhaps the same judgment could be applied to the Reformation as well, treating the political factors as important accidentals.

Without the sixteenth-century Reformation and seventeenth-century Puritanism, there could have been no eighteenth-century Revival. In the same way the nineteenth-century Awakening was dependent upon its predecessors in kind and in time. All major movements were strikingly similar in their duality of effects, having been at once intensely radical and intensely reactionary. They were *radical* in their liberating power, unleashing forces for the greater emancipation of mankind: and they were *reactionary* in their varying emphasis and advocacy of a return to the ancient standards of New Testament Christianity. All these movements thus bear witness to the unchanging verities and ever-changing potentialities of the everlasting Gospel. "The truth shall make you free," said Christ. The Truth is unchanging, though its garments of expression seem different. But spiritual Freedom seems to develop unendingly.

Unlike the Reformation and the Evangelical Revival, the Awakening of 1858 onwards produced no cleavage among Christians, rather sewing together the rent fragments of Evangelical Christianity with the thread of spiritual, if not organic, unity. The Anglo-Scottish Reformation rent the major part of British Christianity from the body of Roman Christianity. The Evangelical Revival separated a considerable part of the religious population from the Church of England. But the Evangelical Awakening of the nineteenth century produced no further divisions, but indicated that the tide in church relations had begun to flow in the other direction.

The unity promoted by the nineteenth-century Awakening was of the spiritual rather than the organic kind. Its co-operation is typified by the interdenominationalism of evangelistic campaigns, of conventions for the deepening of the spiritual life, and of missionary comity rather than a rigid union of differing bodies in one super-organization.

*   *   *   *   *

In the fifteenth century, the Lollard Movement, truly a Revival of Religion, was running its course in England. Originated by Wycliffe, its great contribution was the Bible in the English language, something which has never been lost. The Lollard Revival was followed by Reaction and Persecution, which stamped it out. The kindred Hussite Movement on the Continent had much the same experience.

In the sixteenth century, the Protestant Reformation began. Had Luther been a resident of France or some other centralized monarchy he would have suffered the fate of John Huss, but the fragmentization of Germany saved him.

The Reformation got under way, led by the Reformers in every country affected by it. Its great contribution was the perpetuation of free evangelical churches, unknown for a thousand years. The Protestant Reformation was followed by Reaction, the Counter-Reformation which drove Protestantism from Spain, Portugal, Italy, France and Southern Germany, but which failed to uproot it in Northern Europe and Great Britain.

In the seventeenth century, the Puritan Movement began, paralleled by the Pietistic Movement on the Continent. It was led by great thinkers, and its great contribution appeared to be the development of an evangelical theology. Bunyan, Milton, Baxter and others led the way, and to the great Puritans, Spurgeon declared he owed more than to any other source except the Bible. Puritanism ran its course, was driven overseas to America, and was followed by Reaction, Latitudinarianism.

In the eighteenth century, the First Evangelical Revival began, stirring the Dutch Reformed and Presbyterians of the Middle Atlantic colonies, then the Baptists of Virginia, then the Congregationalists of New England under Edwards, then crossing the Atlantic to move the Wesleys and Whitefield and set in motion the Evangelical Movement in the Church of England and the other denominations, besides raising up the new denomination, the Methodists. Its great contribution was evangelical experience, for Wesley and Whitefield and all the revivalists insisted upon a personal knowledge of Jesus Christ. Evangelical Revival was followed by Reaction, Deism and kindred errors.

In the nineteenth century, the Second Evangelical Awakening began in 1858, spreading all over the world. Its great contribution was evangelical action, and it produced a flock of great leaders, Moody, Hudson Taylor, William Booth, etc., who extended its work for fifty years, from 1858 until 1908. Beginning with a spirit of prayer and conviction of sin, it continued with an emphasis upon two great doctrines, the authority of the Scriptures and the recognition of the spiritual unity of all believers in Christ. Reaction, already developing in the 1860s, took the place of Revival after 1908. Militant Modernism, a denial of the authority of the Scriptures, rode rampant throughout Christendom and a strong counteraction, Fighting Fundamentalism, supplanted the earlier evangelicalism of Moody, and began to nullify the spiritual unity of all believers in Christ. The nineteenth-century Awakening lasted for a jubilee of fifty years. Reaction triumphed for forty years in the wilderness, during which a crippled Church witnessed the Humanist heresy drive millions to their doom in the horrible World Wars of the twentieth century.

In the twentieth century, following World War II, Humanism is collapsing, and with it Modernism, which is nothing more than a compromise between Humanism and historic Christianity. In 1948 the Holy Spirit, Who was the author of the previous Great Awakenings, began to give the impulse among ministers, students, evangelists and others, and the Third Evangelical Awakening began in America, the Mid-Twentieth Century Revival. When the Enemy comes in like a flood, the Spirit of the Lord raises up a standard against him.

It is my opinion that now, more than ever, we need a better understanding of true revival and spiritual awakening. This wonderful work by the late Dr. J. Edwin Orr has been out of print and difficult to find for far too long. This edition of *The Second Evangelical Awakening* has been prepared and published with the approval of the family of Dr. Orr. This is a copy of the first popular edition.

Dr. Orr's resources in audio, video, and text are available at:

www.jedwinorr.com

If you have questions or comments, you may send them to me.

David Guzik
david@enduringword.com

CPSIA information can be obtained
at www.ICGtesting.com
Printed in the USA
FSHW02n1655160618
49227FS